ON

NOZICK

Edward Feser
Loyola Marymount University

THOMSON

———————※———————™

WADSWORTH

Australia • Canada • Mexico • Singapore • Spain • United Kingdom • United States

Printed in Canada
1 2 3 4 5 6 7 07 06 05 04 03

Printer: Transcontinental-Louiseville

ISBN: 0-534-25233-8

For more information about our products, contact us at:
Thomson Learning Academic Resource Center
1-800-423-0563

For permission to use material from this text, contact us by:
Phone: **1-800-730-2214**
Fax: **1-800-731-2215**
Web: **www.thomsonrights.com**

Asia
Thomson Learning
5 Shenton Way #01-01
UIC Building
Singapore 068808

Australia/New Zealand
Thomson Learning
102 Dodds Street
Southbank, Victoria 3006
Australia

Canada
Nelson
1120 Birchmount Road
Toronto, Ontario M1K 5G4
Canada

Europe/Middle East/South Africa
Thomson Learning
High Holborn House
50-51 Bedford Row
London WC1R 4LR
United Kingdom

Latin America
Thomson Learning
Seneca, 53
Colonia Polanco
11560 Mexico D.F.
Mexico

Spain/Portugal
Paraninfo Thomson Learning
Calle/Magallanes, 25
28015 Madrid, Spain

Table of Contents

Preface

Sadly, Robert Nozick passed away while this book was being written. His untimely death (from the stomach cancer he had been battling for years) was made all the more poignant by the fact that a renaissance of interest in his work appears recently to have gotten underway. Two important volumes on Nozick – those of Lacey (2001) and Schmidtz (2002) – had appeared around the time of his death, and with the release in 2001 of the major work *Invariances: The Structure of the Objective World*, Nozick seemed poised once again for a round of vigorous philosophical controversy (the first round having been occasioned in 1974 by *Anarchy, State, and Utopia*, the work for which Nozick is best known). It is my hope that the present essay will, in its own small way, contribute to advancing the study of the work of this important thinker.

Participation in a Liberty Fund colloquium on Nozick's *Anarchy, State, and Utopia* in Bozeman, Montana from May 30 to June 2 of 2002 helped to sharpen my thoughts on Nozick's political philosophy. I thank the Liberty Fund, conference director Eric Mack, and the other attendees for stimulating discussion. I also thank the Social Philosophy and Policy Center at Bowling Green State University in Bowling Green, Ohio, and its directors Fred D. Miller, Jr., Ellen Frankel Paul, and Jeffrey Paul, for hosting me as a Visiting Scholar at the Center during the summer of 2002, during which time this book was completed. Assistant director Travis Cook and the Center staff also provided invaluable assistance.

Portions of chapters 3 and 5 are reprinted with kind permission of the publisher from *The Independent Review: A Journal of Political Economy* (Fall 2000, vol. V, no. 2, pp. 220, 221, 227, 228, 231). © Copyright 2000, The Independent Institute, 100 Swan Way, Oakland, California 94621-1428; www.independent.org. I thank Robert Higgs, the editor of that journal, and Loren Lomasky, for helpful comments on an early draft of the excerpted article.

I also thank Daniel Kolak, editor of the Wadsworth Philosophers Series, for the opportunity to write this book.

Last and very far from least I thank my beloved wife Rachel for her patience and love during the writing of this book. It is to her that the book is dedicated.

1

Nozick and Political Philosophy

Philosophers have frequently taken an interest in politics. Plato's *Republic*, Aristotle's *Politics*, St. Augustine's *City of God*, Machiavelli's *The Prince*, Hobbes's *Leviathan*, Rousseau's *On the Social Contract*, Locke's *Two Treatises on Government*, Burke's *Reflections on the Revolution in France*, Hegel's *Philosophy of Right*, Marx's *Capital* and Mill's *On Liberty* have become classics of political thought every bit as important and influential as the great works of metaphysics and epistemology. Indeed, perhaps more influential, at least in the realm of practical affairs: the American, French, and Russian revolutions are just three of the more dramatic examples of the ways in which the ideas of philosophers have had tangible political impact, for good and ill.

Curiously, this concern with politics disappeared almost entirely within the Anglo-American analytic tradition in philosophy in the early 20th century. This tradition was for the first two-thirds of that century dominated by two schools of thought, the logical positivism of the Vienna Circle and the so-called "therapeutic positivism" associated with the Cambridge University-based Austrian philosopher Ludwig Wittgenstein and Oxford's "ordinary language" philosophers. The former school took all meaningful statements to be either analytic or empirically verifiable, which entailed that genuine assertions could be made only within the boundaries of mathematics and logic on the one hand or science on the other. All other statements – including those about ethics, theology, metaphysics, and indeed most of the traditional problems of philosophy – were regarded as meaningless pseudo-statements, devoid of cognitive content. The latter school also dismissed traditional philosophical problems as pseudo-problems, though it rested this dismissal not on the logical positivists' "principle of verification," but rather on the notion that philosophical problems arise out of a failure to pay careful attention to the way language actually functions in everyday contexts. Getting clear on the role played by words like "mind," "body," "knowledge," "free will," etc. in ordinary discourse would, it was claimed, enable us to see that there really need be no difficulty in understanding the relationship between mind and body, the manner in which we can come to have knowledge about the external world, whether or not we ever truly act freely, or any of the other matters philosophers have historically taken to be deeply mysterious.

This, at any rate, is the conventional account (greatly oversimplified) of the early history of analytic philosophy. And among the consequences of the intellectual trends it describes was the virtual death of political philosophy as an active sub-discipline. For the logical positivist, statements about justice, the ideal society, the nature of rights, our obligations to obey the state, and so forth, being neither analytically true nor empirically verifiable, were simply without meaning; for the ordinary language analyst, they were statements that may have a legitimate role within everyday political debate, but also had to be evaluated solely within that context, with the philosopher per se having nothing necessarily more enlightening to say about them than the average citizen or statesman.

But logical positivism and its "therapeutic" counterpart eventually died out as significant movements, for reasons that are complex. Suffice it for our purposes to note that the principle of verifiability, being itself neither analytically true nor empirically verifiable, was bound to run its proponents into trouble sooner or later, while the analysis of ordinary language, though often bringing clarity to the discussion of philosophical problems, had a notorious tendency to sidestep those problems rather than solve (or dissolve) them. It really does one no good to be told that in ordinary contexts being "free" to act just means not acting under duress or under the influence of drugs or hypnosis, when the philosophical problem of free will concerns whether even acts that are free in that sense are still acts one could, given heredity, environment, and the network of physical causes described by science, have avoided doing. Nor does it help, in

2

determining what justice demands or what rights are and where they come from, to look at how ordinary voters and politicians use the terms "justice" and "rights," when such people disagree among themselves about these matters.

The demise of these intellectual movements thus, unsurprisingly, brought about a renaissance of substantive political thought within the analytic tradition. But the revived discipline was only strengthened by the schools of thought that had for so long driven it into dormancy, for though the specific doctrines advocated by logical positivists and ordinary language analysts have been largely abandoned, their methods and intellectual ideals – in particular, an insistence on detailed argumentation, clarity of expression, analytic rigor, and appreciation for relevant empirical issues – have had a lasting and salutary influence on Anglo-American philosophy, including political philosophy. John Rawls's seminal *A Theory of Justice* (1971) is generally regarded as the take-off point of the revival of political philosophy in the analytic tradition. Rawls's work was notable for bringing to the field the kind of precision and application of empirical considerations (such as those drawn from economics) that have become the hallmarks of that tradition. It was notable also for its original and sophisticated defense of modern liberalism, a political philosophy that had had a tremendous practical impact on American life in the twentieth century, particularly with Franklin Roosevelt's New Deal and Lyndon Johnson's Great Society. Coming along in the wake of the Great Society, as liberalism was at the height of its influence, and just as the analytic tradition in philosophy, by then dominant in America, was beginning to move beyond its positivist roots, Rawls's book could hardly fail to become a classic.

It was not the only classic in political philosophy to emerge from this period. Robert Nozick (1938-2002) was a younger colleague of Rawls's at Harvard University. He had studied at Princeton with Carl Hempel, a giant of the logical positivist tradition, and while still in graduate school had gained a reputation for the brilliance with which he had tackled philosophical problems in the philosophy of science and decision theory, traditional areas of analytic interest. His fame would spread beyond the community of Ivy League philosophers and into the wider intellectual world, however, with the publication in 1974 of *Anarchy, State, and Utopia*, a work of political philosophy that has become, with Rawls's work, one of the two most influential books in that field of the 20th century. That book is the focus of the present essay.

Like Rawls's book, Nozick's applied the methods of analytic

thought to a set of issues earlier analytic philosophers had largely ignored – and it did so with a greater panache than was usually to be found in works of analytic philosophy, and certainly in Rawls's decidedly genteel and dryly academic writings. *Anarchy, State and Utopia* notoriously abounds with witticisms, engagingly bizarre examples, and fascinating digressions, which augment the book's rigorous and often ingenious argumentation and conceptual analysis. Equally notoriously, though, it defends a political philosophy which stands at 180 degrees from Rawls's – a philosophy known as *libertarianism*, which holds that the most free, just, and prosperous society is one characterized by strictly limited government and a free market or capitalist economic order, rather than the paternalistic welfare state associated with Rawlsian liberalism. If Rawls's position reflected the dominance of left-of-center political ideals in American life from the 30's through the early 70's, Nozick's foreshadowed the revival of right-of-center politics that began with the tax revolts of the late 70's and the election of Ronald Reagan to the presidency in 1980. As representatives of the mainstream Left and Right within late 20th century American politics, Rawls and Nozick soon became, in the words of economist Jude Wanniski, the "yin and yang" of contemporary political philosophy (quoted in Rothenberg 1983).

Nozick's position, though reflective of an important and influential way of thinking in everyday political life, was one which nevertheless had very few defenders within academic philosophy, dominated then (as now) by various left-wing points of view. It was, however, not a position that simply fell out of the sky from nowhere. Views similar to those of Nozick had over the centuries been defended within political philosophy by such thinkers as John Locke, John Stuart Mill, and Herbert Spencer, within economics by the Late Scholastic writers of the Spanish "School of Salamanca" and by Adam Smith, and had underlain the thinking of Thomas Jefferson, James Madison, and many of the other American Founding Fathers. And while the ideals of limited government and the free market had been overshadowed in the late 19th century by the rise of socialism and egalitarian liberalism, they had nevertheless been kept alive and developed in the 20th by such writers as the economists Ludwig von Mises, F.A. Hayek, and Milton Friedman and the novelist and philosopher Ayn Rand. It was this tradition of thought, however far outside the radar range of most mid 20th century analytic philosophers, that had formed Nozick's outlook, and an important part of his achievement is to have brought it back into the mainstream of academic political philosophy.

Such a tradition might seem an unlikely influence on a thinker of

Nozick's background – a Jewish intellectual from Brooklyn, whose career had begun in the turbulent 60's, the era of the Great Society, anti-Vietnam War protests, and the counterculture of the hippies and Woodstock. Indeed, Nozick had started out on the political Left, as a socialist. His interest in libertarian ideas was originally a purely negative one – he had been led by his initial encounter with them to "take [them] seriously enough to want to refute them, and so to pursue the subject further" (Nozick 1974, xvi). But what followed was conversion rather than refutation. As Nozick recounted his experience:

> While in graduate school I encountered the writings of Friedrich Hayek and Ludwig von Mises, which shook me out of my then socialist beliefs. There was Hayek's book of essays, *Individualism and Economic Order*, and Mises's wide-ranging and unsettling *Socialism*, which showed me I had not thought through any details – economic, social, or cultural – of how socialism would work. One of their arguments in particular, about the impossibility of rational economic calculation under socialism, dumbfounded me. Whether or not the argument was ultimately judged to be correct, it was *amazing*, something I never would have thought of in a million years. (Nozick 1986, 187)

If the economic arguments of Mises and Hayek were what awakened Nozick from his dogmatic slumbers (to allude to Kant's famous description of the effect Hume's writings had on him), it was a decidedly philosophical set of ideas that was to form the foundation of his own version of libertarianism. For Nozick rests his position on the concept of *natural rights*, rights individuals have by nature rather than by convention or the decree of some authority, and he argues that the extremely limited government and capitalist economic system he advocates follow from a consistent respect for these rights. In particular, he argues that individual rights to life, liberty, and property give individuals *entitlements* over the fruits of their labor, such that the state cannot justly redistribute wealth for purposes of social welfare – contrary to the socialist and egalitarian liberal theories of distributive justice dominant in political thinking at the time Nozick wrote. The notion of rights is a familiar component of everyday political debate, and it has had a long and distinguished history in political philosophy; but like political philosophy in general and libertarianism in particular, it had fallen out of favor in early 20th century intellectual life. A lasting effect of Nozick's work has been to put the idea of rights back into play in mainstream philosophy, and even philosophers unsympathetic to

Nozick's overall conclusions nevertheless acknowledge that a doctrine of rights of *some* sort or other is essential to a complete political philosophy.

Nozick's contribution to political thought, then, includes this reintroduction of the concept of natural rights, along with the "entitlement" conception of justice he bases upon it, which has become one of the standard positions on the issue of distributive justice with which every political philosopher must come to terms. These elements, along with the role he played in reviving general political philosophy as an active field of research and in bringing libertarianism into mainstream discussion, together constitute a significant achievement.

Still, at least this last element, it must frankly be acknowledged, has not been warmly received by all political philosophers. As Jonathan Wolff has written of the reception of Nozick's libertarianism in the 70's and early 80's, students of political thought typically either "thought its conclusions so repugnant that it should not be taken seriously as political philosophy at all, or they thought its conclusions so repugnant that it was vital (but not very difficult) to show how it fails" (1991, vii). The contemporary university, as the reader no doubt does not need to be told, is hardly a hotbed of sympathy for the ideals of limited government, capitalism, or any other characteristically "right-wing" cause. Students are accustomed today to the assumption that such views are indefensible and unworthy of consideration – or in any case, that they are not considered, much less defended, by many of their peers or professors. Nozick recognizes this, noting that, in taking the position he does, "I run the risk of offending doubly: for the position expounded, and for the fact that I produce reasons to support this position" (1974, x).

Perhaps I should say at the outset that I do not share this (rather typical) negative attitude toward the sort of views defended by Nozick; indeed, my own view is the one that Wolff perceives to be increasingly common since the late 80's – the view that "broadly speaking, Nozick is right" (1991, vii). Accordingly, this book promises to be something unique in the literature on Nozick – a more or less *sympathetic* introduction to his political philosophy. Sympathetic but not uncritical; for we shall consider the objections of Nozick's various detractors, as well as note the respects in which Nozick's position may be in need of supplementation or modification. But we shall also see that those critics have by no means refuted Nozick, and that the gaps in his position are readily repaired – so that the case that Nozick makes for libertarianism stands as formidable indeed.

Readers already somewhat familiar with Nozick and the literature his work has generated may wonder whether in defending Nozick, I might have to take on the man himself; for in some of his later writings, Nozick expressed the thought that "the libertarian position I once propounded now seems to me seriously inadequate" (1989, 286-7; see also Nozick 1993, 32), and the rumor soon went out that "now he is no longer a libertarian" (Wolff 1991, 156). Evaluating this rumor had for some time been problematic, however, in that Nozick tended (notoriously) to refrain from answering his critics, and indeed from writing much of anything at all on political philosophy after the appearance of *Anarchy, State, and Utopia.* His writings from the 80's and 90's never touch on these issues more than tangentially, and when they do, they fail to do more than hint in the vaguest way at what precisely Nozick had rejected of his earlier views.

In any case, Nozick had, just prior to his untimely death, at last revisited these issues, briefly endorsing in his final work *Invariances* something like his earlier libertarian theory of rights (2001, 281-282). And in response to an interviewer inquiring whether he would still apply to himself the description "libertarian," he answered:

> Yes. But I never stopped self-applying it. What I was really saying in *The Examined Life* was that I was no longer as hardcore a libertarian as I had been before. But the rumors of my deviation (or apostasy!) from libertarianism were much exaggerated. (Sanchez 2001)

Perhaps more startling, though, than his sometimes ambiguous statements concerning his libertarianism is Nozick's disavowal of the label "political philosopher," despite the fact that his political philosophy is what he is best known for. But then, *Anarchy, State and Utopia* was, not the summation of his life's work, but the beginning of it. Five more books followed, and all dealt primarily with matters other than politics, in many cases making major contributions to other areas of philosophical concern. The massive *Philosophical Explanations* (1981) deals in depth and with originality with the problems of personal identity, free will, ethics, the meaning of life, the existence of something rather than nothing, and the possibility of knowledge; and the views expressed in this book, especially those concerning epistemology, have spawned a large literature of their own. *The Examined Life* (1989), a less formal, semi-popular series of "philosophical meditations," addresses themes as diverse as God, death, love, sex, the Holocaust, wisdom, and children. *The Nature of Rationality* (1993), a more rigorous and systematic work, returns to the interests of Nozick's pre-*Anarchy, State and Utopia* days (and to the subject of his Ph.D. dissertation "The Normative Theory of Individual Choice," published in book form in 1990), the theory of rational decision. *Socratic Puzzles* (1997) collects a number of previously published essays – technical pieces on decision theory, philosophy of science, ethics and political philosophy, popular articles and book reviews, and even a few short stories. And Nozick's last book, the aforementioned *Invariances*, presents an ambitious theory of objective reality inspired by considerations drawn from physics, evolutionary biology, economics and neuroscience, and which ties together and attempts to solve such traditional philosophical puzzles as the nature of truth, necessity vs. contingency, the mind-body problem, and the rational status of moral values.

With such a diverse set of interests, it is understandable why Nozick should have found it irksome being pigeonholed as a political philosopher. It is also understandable why he did not respond to the vast literature engendered by his work in political philosophy. "I did not want to spend the rest of my life writing 'The Son of Anarchy, State, and Utopia,' 'The Return of the Son of...,' etc." he wrote; " I had other philosophical questions to think about..." (1997, 2). Nor had he responded to the literatures generated by his work on those other questions. Nozick's tendency was to focus intensely for a time on a particular set of philosophical issues, develop and publish a detailed, rigorously defended, and original position on those issues, and then move on to some new set of problems, almost without looking back.

This being so, the question naturally arises why most books on Nozick – including this one – focus almost exclusively on his libertarian political theory. But the very diversity of Nozick's writings is itself part of the reason: Unlike the oeuvres produced by so many of the great philosophers of history, Nozick's body of work does not comprise an overall system that weaves together into one grand vision all of reality, inclusive of metaphysics, epistemology, ethics, politics, religion, and so forth. In this he is very much in line with the piecemeal and "down to earth" approach to philosophy typical of the Anglo-American analytic tradition his work grew out of. And his philosophy is thus not easily susceptible of a unified presentation and summation in an introductory work (though see Lacey 2001 for a recent attempt at something along these lines).

The more important reason, however, is simply the intrinsic and unique significance of Nozick's contribution to political philosophy. Nozick's contributions to other fields are without a doubt important, even brilliant (indeed, Nozick's reputation as a polymath was matched by his reputation for brilliance), but it is his defense of libertarianism that has proved to be the most original, influential, and certainly controversial aspect of his work. The aim of this book is to show how powerful that defense is. And in doing so we shall see also how Nozick's political philosophy fits into a larger, complex tradition of political thought that preceded Nozick and has carried on beyond the point at which he left it – though carried on in a way that would not have been possible without him. Too many of Nozick's critics treat *Anarchy, State, and Utopia* the way Nozick says socialists and egalitarian liberals treat the wealth that individuals have produced through their own creative efforts – as if it appeared from nowhere, or simply fell from the sky like "manna from heaven" (1974, 219). Ignoring the larger tradition to which Nozick's position belongs, they thus tend to regard that position as, though ingeniously presented, nevertheless idiosyncratic and easily dismissed. As we shall see, it is neither.

2
Libertarianism

What libertarianism is (and what it isn't)

Libertarianism is the doctrine that the highest political value is the freedom of the individual to exercise his rights to life, liberty, and property as he sees fit, consistently with a similar exercise of such rights on the part of all other individuals. It holds, accordingly, that the power of the state over the individual ought to be severely restricted, with the legitimate functions of government limited more or less to the protection of the rights mentioned. Other tasks now typically carried out by the state – education, social insurance, looking after the indigent, and so forth – ought instead to be taken care of by private individuals and organizations cooperating through voluntary transactions in a free market or capitalist economy.

That, at any rate, is a reasonable first approximation to what libertarianism is; as we'll see, things get a bit more complicated when we consider the different ways in which the libertarian position has been fleshed out and argued for. We've said enough so far, however, to indicate what libertarianism *isn't*. It is not, and does not claim to be, a completely *general* social philosophy, i.e. one that attempts to provide answers to every important question that could be asked about the human situation. In particular, it does *not* (as its critics on the Left often assume) claim that the free market meets every human need, nor does it hold that all human relations ought to be modeled on the relationship between buyer and seller. Neither is libertarianism a completely general *moral* philosophy. It does not (as critics on the

10

Right often suppose) claim that *all* moral questions are ultimately questions about rights, and it does not hold that advocating (as libertarians generally do) the decriminalization of drug use and the like entails that one must regard such activity as morally defensible.

Libertarianism, that is to say, is a doctrine with a very narrow scope. It concerns itself *only* with the issue of the proper role of government in society, and insists that that role ought to be very small. It is for this reason above all that it favors a capitalist economic order: not because capitalism does everything, or does perfectly the things it does do, but because (libertarians claim) it at least does the things it does better than government can do them. And the things it doesn't do are (libertarians would also claim) things that the government also doesn't do, and that it is dangerous for government to try to do – things, that is, that involve the very deepest of human moral and spiritual needs, things that can be done well only by families and friends, private charitable organizations, religious institutions, and the like. This is also why libertarians take the stand they do on issues concerning so-called "victimless crimes": It is not that libertarians necessarily deny that drug use, prostitution, or whatever, are immoral (some libertarians would deny this, but many would not); the libertarian view is rather that, even if such practices are immoral, the state has no business *enforcing*, through coercion, moral rules against behaviors that hurt only the one practicing them, and violate no one else's rights. The libertarian, then, takes individual liberty to be the highest *political* value; he does not, or at least need not, take it to be the *only* value, or even the highest value, full stop (for there are values other than political values – indeed, part of the problem with other political philosophies, the libertarian would say, is that they fail to see this, and thus illegitimately turn every moral question into a political question).

The varieties of libertarianism

Libertarianism comes in many varieties, and we need to distinguish them if we are to understand the position in general, and Nozick's version in particular. We can distinguish first between three different forms of libertarianism that differ in what we might call strictness or "extremeness" (with "extreme" not intended here as in any way a pejorative description). At the least strict end of the libertarian spectrum stand thinkers like the economists F.A. Hayek (1960) and Milton Friedman (1962), who vigorously defend the free market and

11

the ideal of limited government, and argue that much of what modern governments do in areas like welfare, education, health care, and so forth could be done better in the "private sector," i.e. by private corporations, charities, and individuals. These thinkers would nevertheless allow for a significant role for government in many of these areas: Hayek, for example, though highly critical of the expansive welfare states that have developed in the United States and Western Europe in the last century or so, nevertheless advocated a very minimal, state-administered social safety net for those who are simply incapable of supporting themselves in the market; Friedman advocates, not the outright privatization of public schools, but instead the institution of a "voucher" program whereby the government would provide, with funds raised through taxation, a lump sum for the education of each child, which parents could choose to spend, if they wish (and if they believe their local public school to be substandard) at a private school. To be sure, even these views, though they have had a great influence on politicians of a more conservative bent, would be regarded as fairly startling (and no doubt objectionable) by most liberals; but they do in fact allow for a considerably larger scope for government than most libertarians would find acceptable. We can, if we seek a label for this moderate libertarianism, call it just that: *moderate libertarianism*.

At the other extreme end of the libertarian spectrum stands what is sometimes called *libertarian (or "individualist") anarchism* or, as it is most commonly known, *anarcho-capitalism*. This view, represented by Murray Rothbard (1998) and David Friedman (1989) (son of the moderate libertarian Milton Friedman), holds that there is no legitimate role for the state *at all* – *every* government function, on this view, including even police protection and national defense, can and should be provided by private firms (e.g. private protection agencies operating on a for-profit basis and hired by individuals to enforce their rights to their life, liberty, and property by deterring and punishing violations of those rights). A consistent libertarian, the anarcho-capitalist argues, shouldn't advocate *limited* government – he should advocate the complete *abolition* of government.

In between these two extremes stands what seems commonly to be regarded as the standard or "canonical" version of libertarianism, which holds that there is a proper role for government, but that that role is extremely limited. The state's *only* legitimate function, on this view, is to protect individual rights to life, liberty, and property, by providing its citizens with police protection, national defense, and courts of law to administer justice; anything the state did that went beyond these very narrow functions would be illegitimate, because it would itself involve

12

violating individual rights (by, for example, *forcing* some citizens against their will to help other citizens by taxing them to fund welfare programs). The anarcho-capitalist perhaps goes too far, on this view, but milder versions of libertarianism like those advocated by Hayek, Friedman, and many politicians don't go far enough. This version of libertarianism is often called *minimal state libertarianism* (or "minarchism," as opposed to anarchism), and it is associated with writers like Ayn Rand (1967) and the economist Ludwig von Mises (1978). It is also the version of libertarianism defended by Nozick.

Such, then, are the three versions libertarianism takes. We need also to distinguish, though, between two different sorts of arguments for or defenses of libertarianism, which (following Kukathas and Pettit 1990, 75) we can label *pragmatic* and *principled* defenses. Pragmatic defenses of libertarianism typically proceed by trying to show that the ideals of limited government and the free market championed by libertarians best allow for the realization of values shared by libertarians and non-libertarians alike. The reason why one ought to embrace libertarianism, on this view, is that it *works*: it "delivers the goods," goods everyone seeks to realize – in particular, the goods of economic prosperity for the greatest number of people, individual freedom and the self-reliance and human dignity that are its corollaries – better than any other system does. Pragmatic defenses of libertarianism thus tend to appeal to empirical considerations, eschewing philosophical analysis in favor of economic arguments and historical and sociological studies comparing the results of free-market policies with those of government intervention.

Principled defenses of libertarianism, by contrast, emphasize the *ethical*, and not just the practical, superiority of the libertarian position. A society defined by limited government and the free market are, on this approach, ideals to be worked for not merely on prudential grounds (grounds which, after all, will hardly convince those who don't care about prosperity or individual freedom in the first place), but also (and primarily) because we have a *moral obligation* to work for such a society. Principled defenses of libertarianism thus tend to appeal to philosophical arguments, and to emphasize considerations of justice, rights, and the good life, and not mere economic efficiency.

Now the specific moral arguments given by principled libertarians vary depending on the general approach to moral philosophy taken by a particular libertarian thinker. Some libertarians would appeal to *utilitarianism* – the view (very greatly to oversimplify) that the morally right thing to do to is whatever produces the best consequences (e.g. in terms of the greatest happiness of the greatest number) – and argue that

13

it is precisely a libertarian society which produces the best consequences. (Utilitarian moral arguments for libertarianism thus, for obvious reasons, very quickly reduce to pragmatic arguments of the sort referred to above.) Others would appeal to *contractarianism* – the view (again very greatly to oversimplify) that the morally right thing to do is determined by whatever rules rationally self-interested persons would agree to (or "contract" for) if they could start society from scratch – and argue that rules entailing a libertarian society are precisely the rules that would be chosen. The majority of libertarian philosophers, however, appeal to the idea of *natural rights* – rights that individuals have, in some sense, by *nature* and not just because some government or community has (at its discretion and perhaps temporarily) granted them those rights – and argue that the only system morally compatible with respect for individuals' natural rights to life, liberty, and property is a libertarian one. This is the approach Nozick takes to defending libertarianism.

Pragmatic arguments for libertarianism

Since Nozick's position is the subject of this book, we will accordingly be focusing on the moral arguments, and in particular the natural rights arguments, for libertarianism. Before doing so, though, we need to say a little more about the pragmatic arguments, for two reasons. First, we will have need later on in our discussion of Nozick's views to refer to some of the ideas developed by pragmatic libertarians. Second, a full and fair evaluation of libertarianism can be made only by considering *both* the principled and pragmatic arguments, and even principled libertarians, Nozick included, make their case *in part* on the basis of pragmatic arguments. Some people, when first encountering libertarian arguments, tend even if they find them otherwise powerful to dismiss them as impractical. The suspicion is that even if the libertarian vision of social life free from coercion has its moral advantages, it is unworkable: For in a society with minimal government and a laissez faire capitalist economy, wouldn't there be large-scale poverty and the like? The libertarian answer to that question is an emphatic "No!", and the economic and sociological arguments of pragmatic libertarians are appealed to also by principled libertarians to show that their position is by no means a utopian one. If they are more inclined than their pragmatically-oriented cohorts to shout "Let justice be done though the heavens fall!" they would nevertheless insist that the heavens are, fortunately, in no danger of falling. A libertarian society, they would agree, *really does* "deliver the goods," even if it also, and more importantly, fulfills some rather stringent moral demands. It is, as Nozick puts it, "inspiring as well as right" (1974, ix).

The "invisible hand" of the market

Among the best known, and certainly most important, of the pragmatic defenses of the free market economic system favored by libertarians is that which appeals to the idea of the "invisible hand." This notion, made famous by the 18th-century Scottish economist Adam Smith, concerns the manner in which complex social institutions and states of affairs that might seem on the surface to be realizable only by conscious planning and effort are instead often the unintended and unforeseen results of blind, impersonal processes – *no one* in fact acted intentionally to bring them about, though given the intricate order they exhibit, it is *as if* someone did, *as if* they were the product of some unseen or invisible hand. An obvious example of this sort of phenomenon is known from the biological realm: As evolutionary theory reveals, the extremely complicated organisms and species that inhabit our world, though it seems at first glance that they could have been directly created only by a divine intelligence, can in fact be explained in terms of the unthinking, impersonal processes of genetic mutation and natural selection. In the human realm, we have the example of language, which, for obvious reasons, was not and could not have been consciously designed by human beings, since such conscious design itself presupposes a level of intelligence that only the possession of language makes possible.

A free market economy constitutes another such "invisible hand" process. In such an economic system, individuals seek to gain for themselves by convincing others to participate in free exchanges that both sides take themselves to benefit from – exchanges of labor for wages, of products and services for money, of investment in shares of stock for a share in profits, and so forth. Convincing someone that he *can* indeed benefit from such an exchange with you very often requires, of course, convincing him that he would benefit less from exchanging instead with someone else. Thus the centrality to a free market of *competition* – of workers competing for jobs and higher wages, of firms competing for customers, of entrepreneurs competing for investment capital, etc. Now the conscious aims of actors in such a system are varied: Some wish to work in a particular sort of job because they find

15

it intrinsically fulfilling, others may do so only for the paycheck; some may develop new products and services for the sheer creative joy of it, others merely to attract new customers; some may strive for great wealth so that they may someday engage in great philanthropic enterprises, others for the power and comforts it might bring, still others for the thrill of competition itself. But all (or at any rate almost all), to *some* extent anyway, whatever else may motivate them, seek also to do what is in their own self-interest. This emphatically (and contrary to standard caricatures of the market) does *not* mean that they necessarily do what they do for "selfish" reasons; it means only that, however generous and kind-hearted they are toward others, they also wish to better themselves, to make for themselves and their loved ones a comfortable living, with all that that entails – at the very least a decent home, enough to eat, a good education, some luxuries where possible, some surplus to contribute to religious institutions or charities, and so forth. And in so doing, they will seek to do what is necessary effectively to compete in the marketplace – they will, in short, try to discover what it is that others want and try insofar as they can to be the ones to provide it. And if what people want is food and housing, or cars and televisions, or books and music recordings, or computers and other electronic gadgets, or whatever, there will thus be a great many people who, out of a concern for their *own* well-being, will try to *supply* those things for people, and to do so, as far as is possible and profitable, at the price and level of quality people *demand*.

The result of such overall competition is that, generally speaking, and at least in material terms, people in a free market economy get what they want. Music and book lovers get CDs and books, motorists and sitcom enthusiasts get cars and televisions, and almost everyone gets food and housing. They get them, moreover, at ever increasing levels of quality and at ever decreasing prices (as dramatically exemplified by the history of the market in personal computers from the late 70's to the present). And they get things they might never have dreamed they could get as competition gives rise constantly to *innovation*, to improvements in old products and the invention of new ones – some trivial (hula hoops), some enormously enriching (classical music recordings), some life-saving (new medicines and medical procedures). Indeed, they get all this in abundance, as evidenced by the tremendous prosperity, unprecedented in human history, of modern capitalist societies. And while it is of course true that people don't *always* get *exactly* what they want in a free market society, and a few get relatively little, careful consideration of such cases actually *confirms* the general trend described: The vast majority of human

16

beings who have ever lived, and those living today in places where modern capitalist society has not taken root, have been simply too preoccupied scraping together an existence at a meager subsistence level to exhibit the sorts of dissatisfactions characteristic of developed capitalist society – to worry themselves over urban sprawl, say, or the dearth of quality arts programming on television. And the majority (though of course not all) of the "poor" in capitalist societies actually live better than most *kings* who have ever lived, having, as most of them do (and even Charlemagne and Henry VIII did not) automobiles and flush toilets, televisions and VCRs, "fast food" and microwave ovens. (Critics of capitalism thus ought to keep in mind just how *relative* a description "poor" is, and how misleading it is to speak, say, of "poverty" in Africa and the United States as if the same sorts of circumstances existed in both. Whereas the greatest health problem facing the poor in Africa is malnutrition, the greatest health problem facing those counted in government statistics as "poor" in the United States is *obesity*! (Rector 1998))

Note, though, that none of these results came about because anyone *intended* them. In making and selling you groceries or golf clubs, manufacturers and merchants aren't consciously *trying* to help produce an increasingly prosperous state of affairs for all, nor necessarily trying to benefit you personally; they are instead trying to make a profit, and thus help themselves. But in doing so, they, and the millions of other manufacturers, merchants, investors and entrepreneurs in a free market society *also* end up, as a by-product of their self-interested (though, again, *not* necessarily "greedy" or "selfish") behavior, helping *you* and *society as a whole*. The results, though unplanned and unintended, nevertheless come about *as if* they were designed – *as if* some "invisible hand" were guiding everyone, in acting in their own interest, also to act in the interests of all.

The dead hand of the state

That such results could come about without anyone's intending them is only half the irony; for, paradoxical though it might seem, it turns out that the large-scale prosperity, technological innovation, etc. that capitalism makes possible without anyone's trying to produce it *cannot* come about when we *do* try consciously to produce it!

To see *that* this is so, one need look no further than at the history of the communist regimes of the 20th century. Such regimes were, of course, most notable for their unrivalled brutality – it is estimated that

Stalin, Mao, Pol Pot, and the other communist dictators between them murdered upwards of 100 million human beings, to say nothing of the myriad other lesser varieties of "crimes, terror, and repression" that characterized everyday life under these governments (Courtois et al. 1999). But what is relevant here (though, for reasons we'll see later, by no means unrelated) is the economic inefficiency, chronic and large-scale shortages, and resulting mass poverty that characterized these societies. The aim of the socialist economic planners who ran the regimes was consciously to create "workers' paradises" which would outstrip the capitalist world in terms of innovation, production, and prosperity, and without the inequalities typical of free market societies; instead, they created virtual hells on earth, where all (except, of course, the planners themselves) were equal only in their misery. (Libertarian joke: "Communists really must love poor people – after all, they produce so many of them.")

This was no accident. There are reasons *why* the history of communism went the way it did, why it was *bound* to do so. Part of the reason, as is well known, is that in eliminating the profit motive and private ownership of the fruits of one's labor, socialism eliminates the *incentives* that motivate people to produce and innovate: If I'll get just the same as those who work harder or more creatively, if nothing I make belongs to *me* anyway, and if the state guarantees in any case that I'll at least be fed, clothed, and housed (however shabbily), what's the *point* of working hard, or working at all? Why *not* spend the day with a bottle of vodka instead?

But the problem runs deeper than this. Even if, contrary to human nature, everyone had suddenly decided that pleasing Comrade Stalin or Chairman Mao, or the rapture of subordinating one's individual will to that of the People or the Party, or whatever, was incentive enough to try to realize the communist ideal, their efforts would still have failed. For, as Mises (1951) and Hayek (1948) have argued, the impossibility of socialism is an impossibility *in principle*, and specifically an *epistemological* impossibility – fundamentally, the difficulty concerns not motives, but knowledge.

In order for socialist planners to carry out the task of organizing the economic activity of society as a whole, and in particular to determine the most efficient allocation of resources, they need *information* – about the needs and desires of the millions of individuals who make up society, about the abilities and talents of those individuals (which the planners need to draw on), about the location of innumerable and enormously varied resources and the difficulty of acquiring those resources, and so forth. But this information isn't located in any central location or accessible to any one mind. Rather, it is *fragmented* and *dispersed* among millions of individuals, each of whom is familiar with the circumstances of his own time and place, but largely ignorant of the circumstances prevailing in other parts of the economic system. Moreover, this information *cannot* be centralized, cannot be put together for the perusal of a socialist central planning board. For not only is it scattered in such a way that gathering it together is a practical impossibility, but much of it is *fleeting*, that is, it is information about local circumstances that rapidly change, so that even if such information could be gathered, it would largely be obsolete by the time the gathering process was completed. And in addition, much of the relevant knowledge isn't *propositional* knowledge at all, isn't knowledge of data that could be recorded in a ledger or fed into a computer; it is rather what might be called "tacit" knowledge, knowledge embodied in the habits, practices and conventions of everyday economic life, the sort of knowledge – of customers' tastes and needs, of local conditions, of how to deal with sudden and unforeseen problems, of "the way the market is heading," etc. – that an entrepreneur, businessman or merchant has intuitively and only after years of experience. (Think of the distinction between "book-learning" and "know how" available only from hands-on experience, where the latter, by its very nature, cannot be communicated in an explicit way.) What socialist central planners need in order rationally to do their job, then, is something that simply *cannot* be had.

In a competitive market, however, all this inconceivably complex information nevertheless *does* get utilized – in a *decentralized* and spontaneous, *undirected* manner, yet in such a way that an allocation of resources is made that is as efficient *as if* it were planned by some omniscient mind. For the *price system* in such a market serves to distil or encapsulate the information scattered among millions of individual economic actors in such a fashion that they are able to coordinate their efforts, so that account is taken of all the information even though no single individual has access to all of it. For example, such circumstances as an increased demand for tin in one part of the economy, due to its utility in manufacturing some needed product, or the elimination of some source of tin, due, say, to an earthquake which destroys some mining operation, will drive the price of tin upward in such a way that tin users will begin to economize – they will use less of it, find alternatives to it, etc. Contrariwise, a decreased demand for oranges, say, due to a switch of tastes toward grapefruit juice and lemonade, will cause the price of oranges to go down – signaling producers to shift resources to growing less of them and more lemons and grapefruits, and manufacturing fewer orange-based products. And so on and so forth, with regard to *untold millions* of different and varied circumstances, resources, products, producers, and individuals with their idiosyncratic needs and tastes, together comprising a vast system which no one can possibly survey and comprehend in its entirety. In all such cases, a reallocation of resources toward their most efficient uses will take place even though no single individual knows or can know of all the circumstances that led to there being a need for a reallocation – each individual needs to know only that prices have changed, and this signals all individuals to act in a way that it might appear they could act only if directed by some central authority. We have, once again, an example of the "invisible hand" in action.

We also begin to see why the quite visible hand of the state is not likely to be so benign. For an economic system of the sort with which we are familiar in modern industrialized society is simply *too complex* for government to plan, and when it tries to do so, it literally doesn't know what it's doing. The result is *bound* to be chaos, as the finely tuned price mechanism that spontaneously coordinates economic activity and efficiently allocates resources when the market is left alone becomes distorted or destroyed altogether. The government planner is like someone who tries to "improve" upon some isolated and rabbit-free island paradise by introducing some of the cute and cuddly critters – only to find out after it is too late that the rabbits, voracious and reproducing exponentially, quickly destroy most of the native plants, leading to the destruction of the indigenous species who would ordinarily have fed on them. Like such an ecosystem – which is more complex than appears at first glance and than we often can fully comprehend, but which nevertheless functions well, according to impersonal natural processes, when left to itself – the market process also operates according to principles it is naïve to think we can improve upon. We should not have been surprised, then, that the socialist economies of the communist world gradually and relentlessly decayed for decades before finally collapsing altogether in the late 1980's – indeed, Mises and Hayek predicted, as far back as the 1920's, that this is exactly what would happen.

There are other problems with governmental attempts to intervene in the economy, or in other ways to direct the activity of individuals in society. Government officials, no less than businessmen (indeed, no less than *any* of us), seek to do what is in their own self-interest. Such officials, however, are *not* reigned in by the mechanism of competition that puts a check on the self-interest of the businessman. If you are dissatisfied with the service your local grocer gives you, or with the products he sells, you can always take your business elsewhere. Wanting to keep you as a customer, he thus has an incentive to try to please you. The state, though, has no such incentives. It is going to get your money (in taxes) whether you're satisfied with what you get in return for it or not. Nor does the threat of being "voted out" serve as the deterrent one might suppose. With the grocer, no matter how many other people might care to frequent his store, *you* can always go your own way if you see fit; the grocer has to satisfy *you personally* if he wants your business. But an elected official might be able to force his "services" on you – or at least force you to pay for them – whether or not you see fit, as long as he can convince 51% of the *other* voters to side with him. In that case, he won't *need* to satisfy you to get your "business" – he'll get it whether you like it or not.

The state, then, even in a democracy, is nowhere near as responsive to "customer dissatisfaction" as a private firm is. Factor in the circumstances that a voter might like some of a candidate's policies but not all of them – but the voter (and everyone else) must nevertheless take the *whole* package if the candidate wins – and that most voters generally don't have the time, inclination, or ability to understand all the ramifications of these various policies but nevertheless have the same right to vote as voters who *do* understand them, and it becomes even more obvious that the competition between candidates in democratic elections is by no means like competition in the market. Your neighbor may have been a fool to buy that Yugo, but at least *you* don't have to pay for *his* mistake; and you might find Amazon.com's book selection wonderful and their selection of DVD's mediocre, but you can go elsewhere for the latter. If the other voters all choose to enact some foolish or dangerous policy you opposed, however, *you'll* be forced to pay the price for their folly along with them; and if they elect some politician whose foreign policy you like but whose domestic policy you find atrocious, you'll be stuck with both policies all the same.

If elected officials are at best only partially and intermittently responsive to "customer dissatisfaction," government bureaucrats – the unelected, unseen, and largely unnoticed officials who run the day to day apparatus of the state and who remain in power indefinitely as politicians come and go – are almost completely unresponsive to such pressures. Often created to deal with some particular set of problems – concerning education, public health, the environment, or whatever – such bureaucracies are never directly held accountable to voters for *how well* they deal with such problems. Indeed, there is a built-in incentive for them *not* to deal with them *too* well: A bureaucrat who announces that some specific environmental and health problems have actually been *solved* might inadvertently precipitate a reduction in funding to his agency (since it will now presumably need less money) and even worse, a cutback in jobs (maybe even his own!); better to maintain – year after year after year, if job security is what one is after – that the problems are *"being* solved" but that "more funding is needed" to finish the job. And of course, there is for the same reason every incentive to *exaggerate* (and even *manufacture*) problems.

True, private firms also have an incentive to exaggerate and manufacture problems that their products do little to solve – "Use our hair cream and we guarantee you won't go bald!" – but the wary consumer can always ignore such hucksters, and he is in any case unaffected if *others* are taken in by them. By contrast, a government agency which incites needless panic about "acid rain" or (to cite the object of a current wave of hysteria) "second-hand smoke" (Sullum 1998) affects not only ignorant and gullible voters but also informed ones, whose own property may be affected by burdensome and unnecessary regulations; and in any case, when and if the panic is exposed as needless, the bureaucrats running the agency usually pay no price. For *most* voters usually don't care enough about the dubious policy at issue – which typically directly affects only one segment of the population – to raise an outcry; and by election time, when someone could be voted in to reform the agency, the issue has either been forgotten, or has to compete for attention with what most voters take to be more pressing matters (some *new* scare, perhaps). Moreover, the politicians who are the only ones who *could* hold bureaucrats accountable themselves often have strong incentives *not* to do so: For one thing, they too have an interest in exaggerating the problems and "crises" bureaucracies allegedly exist to solve – what better reason to elect them than to "deal" with these problems, usually by adding new agencies or increasing funding to old ones? For another, they are often beholden to the public sector unions that government employees belong to – which grow in size and power as bureaucracies themselves grow, and which will fund only those candidates who will increase their power and decrease their accountability.

Those who bemoan the power of big business are thus naïve if they suppose that government agencies are somehow immune to its corruptions – indeed, they are *less* immune. If you think Microsoft is too powerful, imagine a Microsoft that was able to *force* you to pay for its software, under threat of imprisonment, that was able to *force* (again through imprisonment) other companies not to manufacture any competing software, and that was inclined to change the things about its services *you* didn't like only if you could convince 51% of its other "customers" to make the same complaints (and probably not even then); imagine also that Microsoft has a monopoly not only on software but on dozens of *other* services (social security, postal services, etc.), an army, police, courts of law, and exclusive rights to try and punish you for refusing to comply with its directives – imagine all this, and you've begun to imagine the power of the state. The real Microsoft, on the other hand, is *powerless* compared to all *that* – regardless of how many other people buy its software, if *you* don't like Bill Gates or his products, you can tell him to buzz off and then go by a Mac, and he can't do a thing about it!

The inherent inefficiencies of governmental agencies, and their tendencies to act in ways not in line with – indeed, even contrary to – the reasons for which they were created, are the subject of a whole branch of economic research known as *public choice theory* (Buchanan and Tullock 1962). This research sheds light on why the complaints one hears today about government services – about the post office, public schools, the management of public lands, and so on – are the very same complaints one hears year after year, election cycle after election cycle. The problems never seem to get fixed, and it is no accident that they don't. For as we've seen, given the incentives governing the actions of the state and its officials – incentives very different from those governing the market – there is every reason to *expect* that such problems will arise, and that far from being solved by the state, they are likely to get worse.

Cultural evolution

The market works where the state does not precisely because, unlike the latter, it is governed by an *invisible* hand – by *impersonal* processes that do not, and do not need to, have the knowledge that someone trying to plan an economic system from the top down would have to have (but, as we've seen, cannot have). It is, in that respect, like biological evolution, another "invisible hand"-type process that operates by trial and error and thereby produces an incredibly diverse and complex interconnected system (of life forms, rather than economic transactions), which no human being or committee of human beings could possibly have created. In fact, not only is the market like evolution in that respect, it was (according to free market theorists like Hayek) itself created by a kind of evolutionary process – a process of *cultural* evolution (Hayek 1988; see also Feser forthcoming-a).

23

Social institutions, like biological organisms, are the product of a kind of natural selection. Such institutions consist of systems of rules – of customs, morals, mores, traditions and taboos – that govern the behavior of social groups. These rules may come to be followed for any number of reasons – sometimes because the group decided consciously to adopt them, sometimes because they were foisted upon it; sometimes on well-thought out rational grounds, sometimes for religious or even superstitious reasons. What's more important than why they were adopted, however, are the effects that the following of the rules have on the group over time. Some rules may end up making the group well-adapted to its environment, and these rules will thus tend to preserve the group and cause it to grow and prosper; and the rules themselves will also tend to survive and spread, not only because the group following them thrives, but also because groups following other, less adaptive rules will tend to be displaced by the first group, or will adopt the successful rules of the first group. Correspondingly, rules which turn out to be ill-conducive to group survival will tend over time to die out, since the groups following them will tend themselves to shrink, become impoverished, and die out, or to abandon the rules. Over time, as different groups following different rules compete, those rules which are ill-conducive to prosperity and survival will tend to disappear from human societies, and those which are adaptive and beneficial will tend to prevail – maladaptive rules will, that is, get *selected out* by the process of cultural evolution, and the "fittest" rules (and the societies following them) will be the ones that survive, or at least predominate.

Take the moral rules against murder and stealing, for example. It is obvious that any society which adopts such rules is going to have an advantage over those that allow murder and stealing – societies allowing such practices will simply be too unstable to survive for very long, so that "rules" permitting them are bound to be displaced in human societies by rules forbidding them. A less obvious but more interesting case, however, is provided by the rules that form the basis of free market societies, rules such as the ones requiring respect for private property, freedom of contract, individual liberty, and the rule of law and strict limits on the power of government. It is precisely those societies that have adopted these rules as their core political ideals that have generated the unprecedented wealth and prosperity of the modern, science-and-technology based, industrialized capitalist world; and it is precisely these societies that have thrived, as their rivals – especially communist societies like those of the former Soviet Union and Eastern bloc countries – have languished and even died out.

The lesson of this turn of events, free market advocates conclude, is that the rules governing free market society are simply more conducive to human survival and well-being than alternative rules are. Respect for private property, for example, is essential for any functioning market and the prosperity and innovation the market generates – for if others, including the state, can whenever they feel like it take from people whatever they invent or produce, then people will have no incentive to invent or produce anything. It is essential too for the efficient use of the wealth that the market generates: When no one, or when "everyone" (i.e. the public as a whole) owns something, no one has any incentive to conserve it or use it wisely – hence the tendency for commonly owned resources to become depleted or to fall into decay and disrepair (what economists call the "tragedy of the commons"); but when an individual owns something, he has incentives to use it wisely and efficiently, both economic (the money he can make by renting or cultivating a piece of property, say) and personal (the sense of pride one takes in what is one's own). Private property is also essential for human freedom and dignity, since a society where the state or "society" owns everything and the individual owns nothing is a society where the individual is perpetually at the mercy of the state and its good graces for his very survival, utterly dependent on and enslaved to an authority he can disobey only on pain of starvation. It is no surprise, then, that the communist system, with its contempt for private property and the other rules of the market order, collapsed as it did and that the capitalist world has flourished. The former, organized from the top down, relying on the dead hand of the state, was, from a cultural-evolutionary perspective, simply unfit; the latter, organized on principles allowing for the free play of the invisible hand of the market and all the benefits it makes possible, was bound to be victorious.

Libertarianism and other 'isms'

These pragmatic considerations, even apart from the moral considerations we'll begin to examine shortly, thus provide all by themselves a compelling case for libertarianism, according to its advocates. Individual liberty, private property, and the free market economy that they make possible simply *deliver the goods*, and do so in a way superior to that entailed by non-libertarian institutions.

This is most obvious in the case of *socialism*, which we've already had occasion to mention. Socialism makes equality the primary political value, and since individual human beings, though equal in rights, are manifestly unequal in talents and abilities, family upbringing and opportunities – and thus end up unequal in wealth and income – socialism in its classical form advocates state ownership of the means of production and government control over the economic activity of individuals, with the aim of guaranteeing more equal economic outcomes. It advocates, that is, just the sort of system that was instituted under communism, with disastrous consequences. Given the historical evidence of the failure of socialism, and also the theoretical arguments we've looked at for the impossibility in principle of making socialism work, socialism as an economic doctrine has very few defenders nowadays.

Liberalism is another story, and its relationship to libertarianism is more complicated. There are actually at least two kinds of liberalism, *modern* or *egalitarian liberalism* and *classical liberalism*. Classical liberalism was the view held by such 17th-, 18th-, and 19th-century figures as John Locke, Adam Smith, Thomas Jefferson, Herbert Spencer, and John Stuart Mill, which took individual liberty and limited government to be the chief political values. It was, in other words, more or less identical with what nowadays is called "libertarianism," and libertarians typically see themselves as the true successors of the great classical liberal tradition. By contrast, modern or egalitarian liberalism – the view which these days is usually meant by the expression "liberalism," and which is represented in political philosophy by John Rawls and Ronald Dworkin and in practical politics by the Democratic Party of Franklin Roosevelt and Lyndon Johnson – combines the classical liberal emphasis on liberty with the socialist's concern for equality, and tries to seek a balance between the two. Socialists thus see modern liberals as insufficiently socialist, and libertarians see them as insufficiently "liberal" (in the older, classical sense) or libertarian.

The modern liberal might concede the superiority of the free market in general as a means of organizing society, but would insist that the state must intervene in at least a limited way in the economic system so as to guarantee greater equality, particularly in areas like basic welfare, social insurance, health care, and education. But libertarians would respond that the same principles that make the free market superior to government planning in general also make it superior in these particular cases. State interference with the market distorts its incentives, and particularly the price mechanism, in a way that tends to make things worse rather than better. Minimum wage laws, for instance, artificially raise the cost of labor and thus produce unemployment, which tends disproportionately to impact the poor, who thus have fewer opportunities to find entry-level jobs. And the history of government-run social welfare programs in the United States is largely a history of failure: *Trillions* of dollars were spent on such programs between the advent of the Great Society in the 1960's and the welfare reform measures (supported by libertarians) enacted in the 1990's, and poverty among the underclass only got *worse* and more entrenched (Murray 1994). This was no surprise, libertarians argue, given the aforementioned limits of bureaucracies in dealing with social problems and given that welfare as a (state guaranteed) "right" is bound to foster a psychology of dependence and de facto government subsidizing of irresponsible behavior. Given also that local and private charitable organizations are more likely to have knowledge of the concrete individual circumstances and needs of the indigent than centralized bureaucracies would, we should expect that they would more effectively help the needy than the state can – and indeed, the historical record shows that in the 19th and early 20th centuries, private "mutual aid societies" did just that, before the rise of bureaucratized government social programs wiped them out (Beito 2000).

The state also performs less well in planning for the long term financial security of individuals than they could do themselves, as evidenced by the chronic insolvency of "social security" programs, and their tendency vastly to be outperformed by private investment in the stock market. Citizens would thus be better off with the freedom to take the money the government now uses to fund social insurance programs and invest it *themselves*, in privately run programs *they* judge to be in their long-term self-interest. Socialized medicine is another failure, as evidenced by the constant shortages in manpower and resources and long waiting periods for patient care in countries with state-run health care, like Great Britain. The solution to the problems with semi-socialized (via Medicare and Medicaid) systems like the American health care system is not to *increase* government control – and the inefficiencies, bureaucracy, and distortions of the price mechanism that that entails – but to privatize it altogether. Public education has, precisely as analysts of the nature of government bureaucracy would expect, been a system top heavy with administrators and ridden with incompetent teachers which union-spawned rules have made nearly impossible to fire (Sowell 1993). The cause is the absence of market competition, and the solution is privatization, or at least the institution of voucher programs.

The market-based reforms advocated by libertarians have, in practical politics, often been championed by conservatives, and this brings us to one last position in political philosophy which we need to say something about, namely *conservatism*, a point of view that has a unique relationship to libertarianism. Socialism and egalitarian liberalism are typically classified as "left-wing" positions, but classical liberalism/libertarianism is, with conservatism, generally classified as "right-wing." This might seem odd, given that conservatives stress order, authority, and tradition as the fundamental political principles, and champion traditional moral and religious values. Doesn't the libertarian's emphasis on individual freedom and limited government conflict with all this? In fact it does not. Modern conservatives, going back to Edmund Burke, do indeed seek to defend traditional institutions, but they typically see themselves as defending them *from* the state, rather than by means of the state. Part of the importance of the family and religion is precisely that these "intermediate institutions" shield the individual from the raw power of government, and are better able to fulfill the individual's social needs than the bureaucratic modern state is; the last thing the conservative wants is the state meddling in the affairs of the family and the church, even under the guise of supporting them. Moreover, traditional morality is seen by most conservatives as *undermined* by dependence on the state, not supported by it. Conservatism thus by no means entails commitment to more than a minimal state. Nor is libertarianism by any means necessarily hostile to traditional morality – it holds only that traditional moral rules ought not be enforced *by the state*, not that such rules have no validity. Indeed, Hayek's cultural-evolutionary defense of the traditional institutions of capitalist society was itself inspired by Burke's defense of tradition. And many libertarians (e.g. Murray 1994; Roback-Morse 2001) hold, with conservatives, that only in a society in which the institutions of the family and religion are strong are individuals likely to have the independence of mind and self-sufficiency to resist the ever encroaching tendrils of government into their lives.

While socialism and modern liberalism are inconsistent with libertarianism, then, conservatism, though by no means required by libertarianism – and there are plenty of libertarians who are not conservatives, including Nozick – is nevertheless compatible with it. Indeed, it is through its alliance with conservatism that libertarianism has had its greatest influence on practical politics. And as we shall see, there are respects in which considerations drawn from conservative thinking might serve to bolster Nozick's defense of libertarianism. In any case, it is now time to examine that defense.

3

Individual Rights

The grounds, nature, and implications of rights

Individuals have rights, and there are things no person or group may do to them (without violating their rights). So strong and far-reaching are these rights that they raise the question of what, if anything, the state and its officials may do. How much room do individual rights leave for the state?... Our main conclusions about the state are that a minimal state, limited to the narrow functions of protection against force, theft, fraud, enforcement of contracts, and so on, is justified; that any more extensive state will violate persons' rights not to be forced to do certain things, and is unjustified; and that the minimal state is inspiring as well as right. Two noteworthy implications are that the state may not use its coercive apparatus for the purpose of getting some citizens to aid others, or in order to prohibit activities to people for their *own* good or protection. (Nozick 1974, ix)

With these words, Nozick begins *Anarchy, State, and Utopia,* and also more or less encapsulates the argument of the entire book. As do other libertarians, Nozick would insist that the strictly limited government and free market economic system he favors provide the means for securing the maximum degree of individual freedom and highest level of material well-being for all. But there is an even deeper and more decisive reason for advocating libertarianism: It is simply required by a

29

respect for individual rights. To institute any state more extensive than a minimal state would be flatly *immoral*, for it would necessitate violating the basic human rights to life, liberty, and property. More extensive states, whether they be full-blown socialist "people's republics" or mere social-democratic welfare states, in effect make of their people slaves, and systematically deprive them of their property. True, the slavery and theft may not always be as brutally onerous as exists in the most despotic regimes – those of Hitler, Stalin, Mao, Pol Pot, or Castro, say – but the difference between those and the typical democratic state is only one of (admittedly very great) degree. Violations of rights are *still* violations of rights, even if done gently and imposed by an electoral majority.

This is a radical position, to say the least – and we'll see just *how* radical as we proceed. Why does Nozick adopt it? One possible suggestion is that Nozick is merely appealing to moral beliefs we all have and apply in everyday life, and following them through consistently to their logical conclusion. It is wrong to steal. It is wrong to be a busybody, poking your nose into other people's business and trying to run their lives for them. It is wrong to do these things for any reason, but especially for motives that are *themselves* wrong – out of envy of another person's good fortune, say, or an arrogance that insists that it knows better than you do what's good for you. We would never tolerate such behavior if exhibited by an employer or next-door neighbor. And yet the typical government does these things every day, and gets away with it. It takes people's property from them by force in the form of taxes and uses it for its own purposes; or it gives it to other people who did nothing to earn it themselves, and often justifies such action by appealing to little more than the sheer resentment the "have-nots" often have for the "haves," arguably as a cynical way of buying the votes of the former. It tells people what they can smoke and drink, what foods they can eat, whom they can hire, fire, and rent to, and what they can and cannot do on their own property, apparently on the assumption that government officials – who are, after all, nothing more than people, people just like you and subject to the same weaknesses and temptations (only with greater *power*, and thus capable of greater abuses than you are) – are better able than you are of making decisions about your own life. But by *what right* does it do these things – things that would be unquestionably immoral if done by anyone else?

The answer, in Nozick's view, is emphatically: "By *no* right"! The rights, in fact, are all on the side of the individual, not the government; and we appeal to these rights all the time in everyday political life. We speak, with the *Declaration of Independence*, of "unalienable rights to life, liberty, and the pursuit of happiness." But do these familiar rights really have the apparently extreme implications Nozick takes them to have? Aren't there also rights to things that the government provides that Nozick says it shouldn't, such as welfare? What exactly *are* rights, anyway, and where do they come from?

Kant's Second Categorical Imperative

In articulating his view of the nature and basis of individual rights, Nozick appeals to a fundamental moral principle whose best-known formulation derives from the German philosopher Immanuel Kant (Nozick 1974, 32). Kant is famous for (among many other things) his "Categorical Imperative," the dictum that one ought always to "Act only according to that maxim by which you can at the same time will that it should become a universal law" (Beck 1988, 268). That, in any case, is the first formulation Kant gives the Imperative. A second formulation, more relevant for our purposes, goes as follows: "Act so that you treat humanity, whether in your own person or in that of another, always as an end and never as a means only" (273).

What does this mean? The basic idea is this: An individual human being is not a mere object or thing, nor just an animal, but rather a *person*, a rational being with the capacity for free moral choice, and has, accordingly, a special dignity and value. He has his own purposes and ends, and these must be respected as long as they are consistent with respect for the purposes of others. He is not to be interfered with in the uncompelled choices he makes, as long as he refrains from interfering in the choices made by others. He is above all not to be regarded as a *resource* for others, an instrument that may be used at will for another's purposes. Unlike a piece of unliving matter or an unintelligent brute, he is not properly a means to other people's ends; he is, rather, an end in himself.

That a person cannot be regarded as a means only, but always as an end, entails, in Nozick's view, that a person has certain rights. In particular, he has a right not to be treated in any way that involves using him as a resource for others, or which conflicts with his fundamental autonomy as a free, rational agent. He cannot be killed, or maimed, or stolen from, or taken as a slave. But he also cannot properly be *forced* to use his talents, abilities, and labor to assist others, if he chooses, rightly or wrongly, to refrain from assisting; he cannot be *forced* to refrain from engaging in behaviors others regard as self-destructive, even if they really are self-destructive, if those behaviors do not involve violating anyone else's rights; and so forth.

31

Such a view of human beings is, Nozick argues, the only one which recognizes and respects the "separateness of persons," the fact that we all have our own lives to lead and our own choices to make; we are not mere cells making up the "body" of society, or cogs in a vast social machine (1974, 33). Other moral theories simply fail to take this fact seriously. Classical utilitarianism, for instance, in seeking to maximize "the greatest happiness for the greatest number," leaves open the possibility that some people may appropriately be sacrificed if this will lead to a better result for everyone overall. Utilitarians and other moral theorists frequently speak glibly about the need for us all to subordinate our interests to the "good of society" – as do ordinary politicians, activists, and voters for that matter. But, Nozick says:

> [T]here is no *social entity* with a good that undergoes some sacrifice for its own good. There are only individual people, different individual people, with their own individual lives. Using one of these people for the benefit of others uses him and benefits the others. Nothing more. What happens is that something is done to him for the sake of others. Talk of an overall social good covers this up. (1974, 32-33)

The rights Nozick appeals to in defending the libertarian minimal state, then, follow in his view from nothing less than respect for human dignity, from the basic moral principle that individuals are inviolable, and cannot be sacrificed, against their will, for others' purposes.

The Thesis of Self-Ownership

In addition to this Kantian principle, however, Nozick appeals to another idea which has a long history in libertarian thought and which many commentators (e.g. Cohen 1995, 67; Wolff 1991, 7-8) take to be the more fundamental element of Nozick's system. This is the *thesis of self-ownership*, the notion that each individual human being has complete and absolute ownership of himself – of his body, talents, abilities, and labor (Nozick 1974, 171-172). Or as John Locke, an early proponent of the thesis, put it: "Every man has a property in his own person; this nobody has any right to but himself. The labour of his body and the work of his hands we may say are properly his" (1963). You are, that is to say, your own property; you own yourself.

Probably for most people, this principle will seem just intuitively correct. But for anyone who doubts it, the main argument given in its defense is that unless we assume the truth of the thesis of self-ownership, we have no way of explaining the immorality of many practices we all consider clearly immoral. Take slavery, for example. It is almost universally acknowledged nowadays that slavery is a very great evil. But *why* is it, exactly? It cannot merely be for the reason that slaves are often treated badly. For slaves are sometimes treated very well by their masters, even forming bonds of affection with them; yet surely, it is *still* seriously wrong for even a "kindhearted" master to keep a slave. The only way to explain why this is so is that in making someone a slave, a slave owner simply violates the slave's property rights in himself: No one *else* can properly own you, because *you* already own yourself, and a slave owner is in effect stealing from you.

A more dramatic example sometimes used to illustrate and defend the thesis of self-ownership is that of the "eyeball lottery." Suppose it were possible painlessly to remove one eyeball each from people who have two good ones, and transplant them into patients who were blind, giving them the ability to see. So that as many of the blind as possible could benefit, eyeball donors would be compelled to participate, and to keep the redistribution as fair as possible, the eyeball recipients would be determined by lottery. The result of this would, of course, be that many people who could never otherwise have a chance to see would be able to; and those who had the eyeballs painlessly removed wouldn't lose much, since they'd still have the ability to see with the remaining eyeball. So isn't the eyeball lottery something we should consider? Surely not! Regardless of the good results of such a scheme, the very idea seems monstrous. For it is obviously *wrong* to take people's body parts from them by force, *even if* it is done painlessly and for a good cause. But then why else would this be wrong, if not for the simple reason that people *own* their body parts, and indeed own themselves? Once again, unless we assume the thesis of self-ownership, we have no way of explaining *why* certain things are wrong that clearly are wrong.

The thesis of self-ownership is, then, as plausible and fundamental a moral principle as there could be. But its implications are radical. For if I own myself, it follows that I have a wide range of rights – property rights, in fact. I own my mouth, for example; and that entails that if I decide to use my mouth to say something, then as long as I do not violate anyone else's rights by doing so (e.g. by saying it inside your house, when you haven't given me permission to enter), then I have the *right* to say it, even if it is something you or anyone else, including the government, doesn't want me to say. It's *my mouth*, after all, and I can use it as I wish. (And of course, since your ears are *yours*, you can always take them elsewhere if you don't want to listen to me.) I also own the rest of my body and its parts, which means I can also use them however I wish, even if I choose to use them foolishly. If I want to smoke something you or the government thinks might give me cancer, or eat greasy foods you or the government thinks are prone to give me heart disease, or use certain drugs you or the government thinks it is immoral to use or which haven't been approved by the FDA, then I have the right to do so. It's *my body* after all, not yours and not the government's, and thus if I decide to use it in these ways, that's *my* business. Of course, you or the government may be right – perhaps the things I do with my body really *are* immoral or dangerous. But that's beside the point. The question we're concerned with here is just this: *Who* gets to decide what choices – wise or foolish, moral or immoral – I make with my body? And only one answer is possible: *I* do, precisely because *I'm the rightful owner*. You can try to talk me out of a foolish decision, of course. But if I refuse to listen, you have no right to *force* me not to act on that bad decision.

By the same token, however, if I do make a foolish decision – if I abuse my property (i.e. my body) – that too is *my* problem, not yours. *I* made the bad decision, so *I* have to pay the consequences. I can't force *you* to do it, nor can I expect the government to bail me out. If you freely choose to help me, fine; but if not, I have no business complaining. If I decide to smoke cigarettes, get addicted, and come down with lung cancer, I have no right to force *you* to pay for my medical bills, either directly or through tax-funded, state-run medical insurance. If I become a heroin addict, I have no right to force *you* to pay for drug treatment or clean needles, either directly or through some government rehabilitation program. If I become pregnant after freely engaging in sexual intercourse, I have no right to force *you* to pay to support my child and me, either directly or through welfare benefits. Self-ownership goes hand in hand with *personal responsibility*.

This brings us to the implications of the fact that in owning myself, I also own my abilities, talents, and labor, viz. the effort I exert in working. For if I own these things, then I also own the *products* of my abilities, talents, and labor, that is, whatever wealth I produce in using them. If you have something – a ten dollar bill, say – and freely offer to give it to me in exchange for an hour of work, and I do the work, then the ten dollar bill becomes mine. After all, you *owned* the money and I *owned* the labor, so that we could do anything we liked with them; we decided to exchange them; and so now *I* own the money. That means no one else has a right to it. Thus, if anyone takes that money from me by force, he is *stealing* from me, as surely as if he took one of my body parts – and that includes the government if it takes part of it from me in taxes, even if it intends to use those taxes to help someone who it claims needs the money more than I do.

One might wish to respond to this by suggesting that it is "selfish." But the question of selfishness is a red herring; to raise it is simply to change the subject, which is *not* whether it is right and good for me to help the less fortunate (of course it is), but rather *who gets to decide* if I'll do my duty and help them, and exactly when and how. Does a thief have the right to take my wallet at gunpoint, even if he really intends to use the money for a good cause? Ought I to be accused of "selfishness" if I object? Of course not. So what gives the *state* the right to do what a thief is not allowed to do? Perhaps it *would* be selfish of me not to help a particular individual to whom the government wants to give my tax money; and then again, perhaps not, for I might have other uses for the money which I judge to be better uses. Either way, as it is *my* money, it is *my* decision to make.

In fact, even many of those who would otherwise get my tax money – the fruits of my labor – *benefit* in the long run if the state instead respects everyone's ownership rights over themselves and their labor. For property rights in oneself serve the same economic function that property rights in general do: They encourage the person who owns something to *take care* of his property. If no one owns the pond down the road, no one has any interest in looking after it, and it will likely soon get fished out and polluted. If it becomes "public property," much the same result will occur, since people will tend to take the attitude that looking after it is someone *else's* (i.e. the taxpayer's) problem. If some individual *privately* owns the pond, however, he has an incentive to look after it – to keep fishing down to a sustainable level, and to discourage pollution – because of the *personal* economic interest he has in it. If he fails to manage it well, he, and only he, will pay the price. Similarly, if I do not fully own myself – because the state in effect takes partial "public ownership" of me by taking on the costs for my foolish use of my own body – then I have less of an incentive to look after myself. Someone *else* is paying for the "safety net," after all – why *not* take a few risks? But if I know that I may very well be the only one who pays the penalty for my bad decisions, I'm more likely to think twice. Maybe I *shouldn't* use drugs or sleep around. Maybe I *should* go get a get a job, and save for retirement. If I get in trouble, someone *might* be willing to help me out; but then again, they might *not* be willing (especially if I'm in the habit of doing the same stupid things over and over again), and then I'll really be in a fix.

Whereas guaranteed government assistance for those prone to making foolish choices creates a "moral hazard," then, respecting self-ownership encourages responsible behavior. However real these practical benefits of self-ownership, though, they are of secondary importance to Nozick. The *main* issue is moral, not pragmatic. The bottom line is that it is just *wrong* to treat people as anything but owners of themselves and their labor. It violates their rights.

Lockean Natural Rights

If the thesis of self-ownership serves as a foundation for individual rights, it also helps us elucidate the nature of those rights. We can note first that on Nozick's conception, all rights turn out to be nothing other than *property rights*. The right to free speech, for example, is as we've seen really nothing other than the right to use a certain part of your body, namely your mouth, as you see fit (as well as the right to use the place you're standing as you speak, provided that you either own it as well or have been allowed on the premises by the owner). The right to a free press turns out to be much the same sort of thing. It involves the right to use whatever body parts you use in producing a newspaper, book, pamphlet, or whatever, together with the right to use the paper, printing press, distribution mechanisms, etc. involved in publishing, either because you own these resources or have rented them from someone who does. The right not to be killed, maimed, or kidnapped, is just the right that your property – your body – not be damaged or stolen from you. And so forth.

The notion that all genuine rights are property rights is a very important one in libertarian theory; indeed, many libertarians hold that there is no other way in which the notion of rights can coherently be understood. Rothbard, for example, suggests that the reason controversies about whether rights are "absolute" seem so intractable is precisely because of a failure to understand that all rights are property rights (1998, 113-120). For instance, people often assert that the right to free speech is not absolute, since it would surely be wrong to shout "Fire!" in a crowded theater; and they then conclude that rights in general must be rather loosely defined and subject to any number of qualifications and restrictions by government. Notoriously, where exactly to draw the line in any principled way becomes impossible to determine. But when we understand that there is no "right to free speech" over and above the right to use one's body parts and other property, the difficulties disappear. The reason I cannot shout "Fire!" in a crowded theater is not because rights are less than absolute: I still have an absolute right to use my mouth as I see fit, consistent with your right to use your property as you see fit. But you, having that absolute right to *your* property – a theater, perhaps – also have a right not to allow anyone on it who does not (at least implicitly) promise not to yell

"Fire!" If I really want to yell it, I can still do so – as long as I do it on my own property. In general, the rights we have are just rights to use our property – whether body parts or parts of the external physical world – as we see fit. Thus, if we don't have a property right in some particular thing, we have no right to it at all. If I *don't* own any printing equipment, and no one wants to sell or lend me any, then I will be unable to propagate my views very widely, however much I may freely use my hands to write them out. No right of mine is violated by this, however – there is no "right of free speech" or "right to a free press" that is so violated, because those rights are nothing more than the right to use what I *do* own the way I see fit. As the libertarian philosopher Jan Narveson puts it, "Liberty is Property" (1988, 66).

This brings us to a second feature of Nozick's conception of rights, namely that they are essentially *negative*. A right to X just is a right *not to be hindered* in using something you own, X, as you want to use it. It is *not* a right to have X if you don't already own it and no one wants to give or sell it to you. Your right to your TV set is just your right not to have it damaged or taken from you against your will; it is not a right that someone should buy you a TV set. Your right to life is just the right not to be killed; it is not a right that others should provide you with what you need to live. You own your life, so no one has the right to take it from you. But by the same token, others own their lives, bodies, labor, and the things they produce with their labor, and thus no one has a right to take those things from *them*. In particular, you do not have the right forcibly to take, or have someone else take, other people's resources simply because you want or need them, even if you need them to live (just as you have no right to take their body parts from them even if you needed *those* to live).

A right to what you need in order to live would be a *positive* right – a right to something that someone else must provide you with, as opposed to a (negative) right that someone merely refrain from doing something to you. So-called rights to welfare, health care, education, and the like would be positive rights. But there simply are and can be *no* such fundamental positive rights on a libertarian view. For no one has a basic right against other people that they must provide things for him; to assume otherwise is to assume, in effect, that a person at least partially owns *other* people's property, including their labor. If I claim a right to education, for example, I am in effect claiming that *other* people must provide me with an education – it won't just fall out of the sky, after all – which means I'm claiming a *right* to a part of *their* labor, i.e. whatever labor must go into paying the taxes that fund my state-run school. But no one has a right to anyone else's labor – people own *their own* labor, and cannot morally be forced to give up some of it for others. If you want voluntarily to help me out in paying my tuition, and sign a contract saying you'll do so, that's one thing – in that case, I do have the right to your money, because you've *agreed* to provide it – but if you *don't* agree, I have no such right, and I and the government are stealing from you if we take your money anyway.

Now many rights that people claim to have are positive rights of this sort. The United Nations' Universal Declaration of Human Rights, for example, is filled with claims not only to negative rights, but also to many positive rights – rights to education, health care, even "periodic holidays with pay"! But all such claims are bogus, and the alleged "rights" pure fictions conjured out of thin air. For they conflict with the fundamental rights of self-ownership, and make people slaves to the realization of others' desires and needs.

Being essentially negative, a person's rights function, in Nozick's terminology, as moral *side-constraints* on the actions of others (1974, 28-35). Respecting others' rights, that is, isn't to be understood merely as one goal among others that we might seek to maximize, leaving open the possibility that violating rights in some circumstances for the sake of achieving some other good is an acceptable trade-off. Rather, one's rights constitute a set of absolute restrictions within which all other people must behave with respect to him, and override all considerations of utility or welfare. They lay down the ground rules for our behavior towards others – telling us that, in anything we do, there are certain things we must *not* do. "Side constraints upon action reflect the underlying Kantian principle that individuals are ends and not merely means," Nozick says; "they may not be sacrificed or used for the achieving of other ends without their consent. Individuals are inviolable" (1974, 30-31).

Being inviolable, their rights are also *inviolable* – those rights cannot be overridden for any reason. Nor, given that rights are negative, is there any danger that they might conflict, which would put their inviolability in doubt. If your having a right to X just means that I cannot interfere with your use of X, and my right to Y just means that you cannot interfere with my use of Y, then there is no conflict between our rights: All we're required to do is to leave each other alone. But if I also claim a positive right to Z, and Z requires the use of X, then our rights inevitably will conflict, for the only way I can get Z is if you give me X. Positive rights will generally, and obviously, lead to such conflicts – surely another reason to be suspicious of them. Negative rights, however, will not. Such rights are perfectly *compatible* with one another, and thus with the notion that rights are inviolable.

With its emphasis on self-ownership and property, Nozick's account of rights is very much in the tradition of John Locke, and another aspect of the Lockean conception of rights that Nozick takes over is the notion that rights are *natural*. They are, that is to say, something a person has by nature, not merely as a result of human convention, agreement, state decree, or popular vote. A person, being rational and free by nature, is an end, not a means; he owns himself, and *not* because any other human being gave or sold him himself. Because his essential dignity as an end in himself and a self-owner do not derive from any other person's will, the rights that follow from this dignity and self-ownership do not depend on anyone's will. Those rights therefore cannot be revoked by any individual, government, or electoral majority. They rather serve as the moral standard by which to judge the legitimacy or lack thereof of the actions of individuals, governments, and democratic electorates.

The Minimal State

A judgment on existing governments is indeed clearly entailed by Nozick's conception of rights. Most of what such governments do is, as we've seen, in his view illegitimate. For the only proper functions of government involve the protection of rights. A police force is thus allowable, as is a military, since these are needed to protect individuals from internal and external aggression (though they must be used *only* for these purposes). Courts of law are also necessary, to determine the guilt or innocence of those accused of rights violations and to adjudicate disputes over contracts, which the state can legitimately enforce when the parties to a contract have voluntarily entered into it and thus bound themselves to its terms. Taxes to support these functions of government may justly be raised.

What else can the state do? Nothing. It cannot regulate what its citizens eat, drink, smoke, or otherwise put into their bodies, for as we've seen, this violates their right to do with their bodies as they see fit. It also often violates their right to do with their private property as they see fit – anti-smoking regulations applying to restaurants and other private businesses should therefore be eliminated. For the same reason, the state cannot legitimately enforce codes of morality regarding sexual practices. If you freely consent to engaging in premarital sex or homosexual acts, for instance, then even if many people would regard these things as sinful, they cannot use the government to try to stop you from doing them. At the same time, however, it must be recognized that the state also cannot enforce codes of morality regarding *tolerance*

39

of sexual practices, or tolerance of anything or anyone else for that matter. If some people disapprove of gays or fornicators, and want to avoid associating with them, renting to them, or employing them, then they have the right to do this. That other people are offended by such attitudes, and think all people should approve of "alternative lifestyles," does not give *them* the right to impose their conception of tolerance on those who do not share it.

This illustrates, incidentally, how misleading it is to talk, as many people do, of libertarianism as "fiscally conservative" but "socially liberal." For contrary to a popular misconception, libertarianism does *not* require respect for or approval of "non-traditional lifestyles." It requires only that such practices not be forbidden by *law*. If people want to adopt these lifestyles, the state cannot stop them. But if other people want to criticize and condemn such lifestyles, or try non-coercively to convince people not to engage in them, the state cannot stop *them* either. If libertarianism entails that government cannot impose "right-wing" moral views on people, it also entails that government cannot impose "left-wing" moral views. Respect for individual rights requires the abolition of anti-sodomy laws, anti-miscegenation laws, and state-enforced segregation; but it also requires getting rid of "hate speech" laws, anti-discrimination laws, and state-enforced *integration*. If you want to hire people from all races, religions, and sexual orientations or invite them into your restaurant, that's your business and the government cannot stop you; but by the same token, if someone else wants to *exclude* homosexuals from his organization or keep blacks, whites, or whomever *out* of his restaurant, that's *his* business too and the government cannot stop him either. It's *his property*, after all – he can do with it what he likes.

As we've seen, self-ownership entails that the state can neither force some people against their will to help others, nor force people to do what (it claims) is for their *own* good. Welfare measures must therefore be eliminated, as must "social security" programs and government-run health insurance. For all such measures involve taking people's resources from them against their will – that is, they involve *stealing* from people. But "corporate welfare," i.e. government subsidies to certain industries, must also be abolished, since a private company has no more right to your money than does an individual citizen. Public schools should be privatized, not only because they tend inevitably to exhibit the inefficiency and incompetence that afflict all state-run enterprises, but because it is *immoral* to take some people's money from them against their will in order to educate other people's children. Just as *parents*, not the government and not other citizens, are the ones responsible for feeding and clothing the children they bring into the world, they too are the ones responsible for educating them; they cannot justifiably pass this responsibility off on to others. Moreover, state-run schools inevitably violate the rights of parents to have their children educated as they see fit. When the state decides on the curriculum, it cannot fail to impose some people's values on others: If the government decides that all children must be taught according to the dictates of some particular religion, it violates the rights of parents who do not share that religion; but when it requires that all children must attend sex education classes, be taught to "celebrate" the "diversity" of lifestyles and family forms, etc., it violates the rights of parents who not share *those* values. Public schools, in short, always tend to serve as a means of indoctrination into the prevailing attitudes of whatever political ideology happens to hold power. In a privatized school system, however, parents are free to take their children and tuition money to schools whose curriculum *they* approve of.

For similar reasons, government cannot legitimately fund the arts, museums, or cultural enterprises in general. For in doing so, it once again takes people's money from them against their will. What is worse, however, it often uses that money to fund the propagation of ideas those people find highly offensive. We would all rightly be appalled if the government gave money to a racist artist to paint a picture or write a book that insulted Martin Luther King Jr. We would no doubt say that if someone wants to produce such a work, he should do it with his own money, not the taxpayer's money. But by the same token, religious people are justified in objecting to state funding of art that they regard as blasphemous. If artists want to produce such work, they have every right to do so, using their *own* resources – they do *not* have the right to force *other* people to pay for it through their taxes.

Finally, as might be expected, the government has no right in Nozick's view to control wages, prices, rents, or economic life in general. Part of the reason is, as we've seen, that on the libertarian view, prices determined by free competition allow for the most efficient allocation of resources, and are thus in the long run much more likely than state intervention to produce the greatest possible degree of prosperity for all. But the deeper moral reason has again to do with self-ownership. Since you own yourself and your property, you have the right to work for whatever wages you freely agree to, whether or not they happen to jibe with some minimum wage law; and you have the right to charge (or pay) any price you want for the goods, services, or rental property you rightfully own. The state has no more business interfering with economic life than it does one's personal moral life.

Modern governments in general, since they *do* in fact interfere extensively in individuals' personal and economic lives, are thus open to serious moral criticism. They have *no right* to do these things; indeed, governments have the right *only* to protect the individual rights of their citizens, and when they do more than this, they themselves become violators of rights. They engage, that is, in exactly the sort of criminal behavior they are supposed to prevent.

Rights, in Nozick's view, thus *exhaust* the enforceable obligations we have to one another, i.e. the obligations that the state can justifiably *force* us to fulfill (Wolff 1991, 22). It must always be remembered, though, that Nozick is *not* denying that we have all sorts of other genuine moral obligations to one another, obligations which are no less real simply because the state has no business enforcing them. He does not deny for a moment that we ought to help the needy and ought to live virtuous and responsible lives, nor does he deny that we are deserving of criticism if we fail to do these things. His claim is a claim *only* about the proper functions of government, nothing more. Most of us would agree that being kind and courteous, being faithful to one's spouse, and visiting the sick and elderly are things we all ought to do. But we would also likely agree that it would not be a good idea to pass laws requiring these things, or to punish rude and selfish people or adulterers with jail time. We acknowledge that it is sufficient to enforce these moral requirements by praising those who follow them and criticizing those who do not. We recognize in cases like these that there is no contradiction between believing that something is morally obligatory, and believing also that it ought not be enforced by the state. Nozick is merely saying the same for most of the functions now performed by the state. *Government* ought not do them, he holds, and usually cannot do them as well as individuals and private organizations can anyway; but that does *not* entail that they shouldn't be done at all.

In summary, then, Nozick's conception of the grounds, nature, and implications of individual rights is as follows. People are, as Kant held, ends in themselves, and can never rightfully be treated as means or resources for other's ends; and they own themselves – their bodies, abilities, talents, and labor. Given these basic moral facts, it follows that people have rights to themselves and to the fruits of their labor, rights which:

- are to be understood as being essentially *property* rights
- are *negative* rights to non-interference, not positive rights to other people's resources
- function as *side-constraints* on the behavior of others, moral limits within which all permissible action must take place

42

- are *inviolable* – they cannot be overridden for any reason, even for an alleged "greater good"
- are *compatible* with one another, never leading to conflicts between rights
- are *natural*, not derived from or dependent on any human agreements or conventions
- are *exhaustive*, determining the sole legitimate functions of government.

Given these rights, Nozick argues, a *minimal state* (or "nightwatchman" state) – a state strictly limited to the functions of protecting individuals against force, fraud, and theft, and enforcing contracts – is the only kind of state that can be morally justified.

Libertarianism with foundations

The Priority of Self-Ownership

Nozick, then, draws some rather far-reaching, even startling, conclusions from premises that seem uncontroversial, even obvious. Yet he is sometimes accused of failing to justify the doctrine of rights on which his entire position rests – accused, that is, of presenting a "libertarianism without foundations," in the words of Thomas Nagel (1981). What basis is there for such a charge?

The main reason, no doubt, is simply that although Nozick does appeal in different places in *Anarchy, State, and Utopia* to both the Kantian notion of a person's being an end himself and the idea of self-ownership in defending his belief in natural rights and in criticizing various rival positions in political philosophy, he does not spell out in an explicit and systematic way *precisely* how the individual rights he champions follow from these basic principles. Nor is it entirely clear what relationship he takes these principles to bear to one another. Does he think that they are essentially two ways of saying the same thing? Or does he hold that one of them is more basic than the other, providing its justification? If so, *which* is the more basic – does self-ownership follow from Kant's categorical imperative, or does Kant's principle itself derive from self-ownership?

Nozick does not deal with these questions, nor is it entirely clear from what he does say how he would answer them. In discussing the *general* idea of individual rights as side-constraints on action, he emphasizes the Kantian principle (1974, 30-35); yet in criticizing

43

specific policies of redistributive taxation and the imposition of the will of a democratic majority on the individual, he appeals to self-ownership (1974, 167-174, 276-294). But it seems likely that he takes the former principle to be more fundamental, i.e. that he holds self-ownership to rest on a Kantian respect for persons as ends in themselves.

Taking the Kantian principle to be the more basic one is, however, arguably neither essential to Nozick's position nor even preferable philosophically. Kant's imperative is, to be sure, something with which libertarians cannot fail to be sympathetic; but it is plausible that this is precisely because they are *already* committed to self-ownership. That is to say, it is *because* you own yourself that you are not to be treated as a means, rather than the other way around. As G.A. Cohen, a critic of Nozick, has argued, it seems that someone could violate another's self-ownership without treating him as a means – if I punch you in the nose, I've infringed on your property right in your nose, but I haven't *used* you to accomplish any end (1995, 242). So perhaps one could consistently respect Kant's principle without accepting self-ownership. "By contrast," Cohen says, "if people are self-owners, then they indeed may not be used without their consent" (243). Treating *self-ownership* as more fundamental than, and the basis for, Kant's principle thus seems more defensible.

Admittedly, even this position is not without its problems. Kant himself, after all, seems to have rejected the thesis of self-ownership, though, as Cohen shows, for reasons that are entirely question-begging – Kant assumes, without argument, that only things can be owned, not people (even by themselves) (Cohen 1995, 211-212). Nor does Cohen believe, at the end of the day, that Kant's principle really does follow from self-ownership, for the former, he says, requires not only that people not be used as a means, but also that one take a certain *attitude of regard* for them, which even someone who respects self-ownership could consistently fail to do (240). Not that such objections are conclusive: What *sort* of regard for others must I have in order to treat them as ends, exactly? *Why* isn't simply regarding them as their own property enough? Moreover, perhaps even the idea that self-ownership follows from Kant's principle *can* be salvaged after all. For instance, maybe in punching you in the nose, I really *am* using you as a means – a means of expressing my anger or frustration, say. But *settling* these issues, determining once and for all the *precise* relationship between self-ownership and Kant's principle is surely a tall order – if only because Kant's principle itself, though undoubtedly expressing something of moral profundity, is itself rather *im*precise.

Fortunately for Nozick, however, the thesis of self-ownership seems sufficient all by itself to do the job of serving as a foundation for libertarianism. As central as Kant's principle is *rhetorically* to Nozick's position, it may be *philosophically* inessential. For whether or not Nozick's doctrine of rights follows from Kant's categorical imperative, it *does* appear to follow, in all its details, from self-ownership. Indeed, it seems to follow immediately, even trivially: If I have complete and absolute ownership of myself, then *obviously* I have *property* rights to my life, liberty, talents, abilities, and labor; that's just what it *means* to own myself. Furthermore, since it follows that no one else has property rights to these things of mine, and I own no one else's life, liberty, labor, etc., we can conclude that there are no positive rights to things other people would have to provide me with – rights are entirely *negative* (and thus *compatible*). If others could justifiably override my claim to my life, liberty, labor, etc. – that is, if my rights weren't inviolable side-constraints – it would seem to follow that those others would have at least a partial rightful claim, under some circumstances, to those things, in which case I wouldn't *fully* own myself. Similarly, if my rights are not natural, i.e. if they are granted to me by others under some convention or agreement, then it would again seem to follow that I don't fully own myself – for in that case these *other* people would have the *right* to give me rights over myself, which entails that *they* at least partially own me. But no one even partially owns me, for I entirely own myself – hence my rights really are *natural, inviolable side-constraints*. And as such, even the state can do nothing to violate them – which means, since doing more than protecting my rights *would* violate them, that rights are politically *exhaustive*. So self-ownership and property rights in oneself, with all the features Nozick ascribes to those rights, go hand in hand, as a matter of logical necessity. And as we've seen, the thesis of self-ownership itself seems undeniable. Nozick's conception of individual rights thus seems, contrary to Nagel, to be well-founded indeed.

Cohen's critique

Libertarian philosophers inspired by Nozick have, accordingly, tended to focus on self-ownership rather than a Kantian regard for persons as ends in themselves as the basis for their position. Perhaps more significantly, however, many of Nozick's critics have also acknowledged the thesis of self-ownership to be the primary, and formidable, challenge to anyone who wants to reject libertarianism and its political implications. Cohen, a Marxist philosopher who is perhaps Nozick's most prominent and perceptive critic, goes so far as to concede, after extensive discussion and analysis, that the essentials of Nozick's position more or less really *do* follow from the thesis of self-ownership, that that thesis really *does* have a considerable degree of plausibility, and that the thesis *cannot* in fact be refuted (1995)! Indeed, it is a difficult thesis for left-wing egalitarians in particular to reject, precisely because, as Cohen argues, the Marxist critique of capitalism as involving exploitation *itself* implicitly presupposes self-ownership, and in particular the worker's right to the fruits of his labor. But it turns out that as Nozick holds, it is the *taxation* imposed by the state, and *not* the wages paid for workers' labor by capitalists, that truly violates self-ownership. (We'll see in more detail why this is so in chapter 5.) Self-ownership, Cohen concludes, really is, contrary to leftist assumptions, as inherently and radically inegalitarian a concept as libertarians say it is. Cohen's own strategy against Nozick, then, is not to try positively to refute the thesis of self-ownership, but rather to try merely to show that we don't *have* to accept it after all – to show, that is, that rejecting self-ownership needn't leave us with no basis for objecting to slavery or eyeball redistribution.

Let's focus on Cohen's attempt to explain how the eyeball lottery might be condemned as immoral even if self-ownership is rejected. (See Feser 2000 for criticism of Cohen on slavery.) His approach is to give examples which are similar to the eyeball lottery but which (he alleges) do not imply the thesis of self-ownership, and to argue that the eyeball lottery scenario itself is, despite appearances, also best accounted for in similar, non-self-ownership involving terms. In the first of his examples, we are to imagine a case in which people are born without eyes, and the state provides artificial ones which are implanted at birth and which become workable only when used by an individual from infancy to adulthood (1995, 243-244). Suppose that occasionally an adult, through no fault of his own, loses his artificial eyes and the state takes one from someone else to give to him (since only ones used until adulthood are of any use). Surely we'd object to this just as strenuously as to the eyeball lottery case. But there's no question of these individuals owning these artificial eyes, since the state may well retain ownership of them. So our objecting to the practice must have nothing to do with ownership, but instead be due to discomfort with the excessive interference in people's lives this practice would involve; and the same can plausibly be said of the original eyeball lottery case. Thus we can object to eyeball redistribution, Cohen concludes, even if we reject the thesis of self-ownership.

The problem with this response is that it just isn't obvious that serious interference with people's lives is *all* we object to in eyeball lottery-type cases. Suppose someone was unknowingly the recipient of an eye stolen from someone else, and the original owner demanded that the eye be returned to him. Surely, however much we sympathized with the unwitting transplantee, we'd grant that he should give up the eye to the original owner. Both parties will have had their lives radically interfered with, but it's nevertheless clear that one has suffered a greater wrong, and surely the reason why is that he's the *owner* of the eye. It even seems plausible that Cohen's example is at least *slightly* less horrific than the eyeball lottery scenario, precisely because these people were granted their eyes at the discretion of the state, which thus has some say over who gets them and under what terms – one feels like saying: "Well, they *are* the *state's* artificial eyes, I suppose, so perhaps it's acting within its rights; but *still...*" But then there seems to be nothing to explain the difference between the two cases unless we assume that the reason the original eyeball lottery example is (at least slightly) more horrific is that people are the rightful *owners* of their body parts.

Cohen's other example pictures newborn infants as receiving eyes when passing under "ocular trees" on which eyes grow and from which they fall – most infants anyway, but not all, as some unluckily pass under the trees when nothing falls and thus receive no eyes (244). He implies that no one, neither lucky eyeball recipients nor the state, would own the eyes in this case, but that we'd still object to eyeball redistribution anyway, in which case it isn't self-ownership that we're committed to in rejecting such redistribution. But this example is ambiguous. If we think of the ocular trees as easily manipulable external natural resources that can come to be owned (e.g. by the state), as other natural resources are, then the scenario is more or less identical to Cohen's first example, and has the same problems; but if we think of the trees instead on the model of the genetic factors responsible for eyes in the actual world, or even as similar to conditions in the womb, etc., then the scenario is more or less identical to the original eyeball lottery example, in which case it gives no non-question-begging support to the notion that we needn't account for the immorality of that example in terms of self-ownership.

Consider also that, whatever one thinks of Cohen's examples, there are other ones that clearly cannot be accounted for except in terms of self-ownership. Suppose someone is in a coma and will *never know* that one of his eyeballs has been removed – wouldn't taking it still be immoral? What if we know that he will wake up someday, but that (due to brain damage) he'll be blind anyway – should we take out one or both eyeballs and replace them with artificial ones, so that he'll

47

never be the wiser? Surely not. But the reason why not cannot be because we'd be severely interfering with his life, because we *wouldn't* be. The only possible explanation for the evil of such eyeball removal, then, seems to be one in terms of self-ownership: They're *his eyes*, period, *whether or not* they'll ever be of use to him and *whether or not* he'd miss them.

Deeper foundations?

So the thesis of self-ownership, despite Cohen's best efforts to side-step it, seems morally unavoidable, and thus serves as a firm foundation for Nozick's libertarianism. But many libertarian philosophers have sought to hedge their bets by digging deeper, providing even firmer foundations for their position by arguing for self-ownership in terms of yet more fundamental moral principles. It is not *merely* because it accounts for the evils of slavery, eyeball redistribution, and the like that we ought to accept the thesis of self-ownership, these theorists would argue. Self-ownership follows from much more general facts about the human moral situation.

How these more general facts are to be understood varies with the general position in moral philosophy advocated by the libertarian thinker in question. Some libertarian writers, as we've noted already, take a *contractarian* approach to ethics (Buchanan 1975; Narveson 1988). For them, all morality rests on an implicit social contract between the members of society. Only those moral rules that would be agreed to by all rationally self-interested persons can be regarded as binding – indeed, their mutual agreement is what *makes* the rules specifically *moral* rules, and thus binding, at all. Libertarianism arguably follows automatically from this: Not all rationally self-interested persons would agree to rules guaranteeing welfare or equality as a matter of right; but they would agree to the rights comprising self-ownership. Self-ownership, then, derives from the very social contract that supports *all* morality. Whether this sort of argument succeeds depends, of course, on whether contractarianism in general is a defensible moral position, and whether libertarianism really does follow from it. John Rawls, being not only a liberal egalitarian but also a contractarian of sorts, would disagree with the latter claim – though as we'll see in chapter 5, his position has problems of its own. Nozick himself, though he does, as will become evident in the next chapter, take the minimal state to result in part from a kind of contract, is not a contractarian per se – for him, as for Locke, our rights do not *follow* from a contract, but *precede* any social contract and provide moral boundaries within which all such contracts must be made. A contractarian approach, then, whatever its merits (which we cannot evaluate here) is not the one most conducive to defending a distinctly Nozickian version of libertarianism.

More hopeful is the strategy, pursued by a large number of libertarian philosophers, of appealing to a broadly *Aristotelian* account of morality (Mack 1981; Machan 1989; Rasmussen and Den Uyl 1991; Smith 1995). On Aristotle's view, the *fundamental* moral question is not "What is the right thing to do?" but rather "What traits of character should I develop?" Only when one has determined what traits these are – that is, what habitual patterns of action count as *virtues* – can one go on to answer the subordinate question of how one ought to act in a particular case (the answer being that one should act the way someone possessing the virtue relevant to that situation would act). What count as the virtues, in turn, are just those qualities most conducive to enabling human beings to fulfill the potentials which distinguish them as the unique sorts of beings they are – those qualities, that is, which best allow human beings to *flourish* given their distinctive *human nature*. Given that human beings are by nature *rational* animals, we can flourish only if we practice those virtues governing practical and theoretical reason. It follows that we have reason to acquire intellectual virtues like truthfulness and practical virtues such as temperance and courage, and to avoid such corresponding vices as licentiousness and cowardice. Given that human beings are also by nature *social* animals, we can only flourish if we practice also those virtues governing interaction with other human beings, so that we have reason to acquire such social virtues as honesty and loyalty. Though the moral life will involve decision-making about what to do in a particular concrete situation, then, it involves more basically the gradual development of a *good character* by the taking on of the virtues and the weeding out of vices – it essentially involves, that is, a process of *self-perfection*.

Only a person who voluntarily decides to do so can carry out this process, however – virtue must be freely chosen if it is truly to count as virtue. Moreover, the *specific* requirements of virtuous behavior depend to a considerable extent on the unique circumstances of the situation and the individual person involved, circumstances knowable only to that person himself in the concrete contexts of moral decision-making. The moral life, then, is only fully possible under conditions wherein the individual is capable of *self-direction* (in Rasmussen and Den Uyl's terms), the absence of coercion and interference from outside forces. Allowing *others* such self-direction is necessary too if the individual is to allow those others also to develop the virtues; and in

49

general, respecting others' autonomy is essential if one is successfully to cooperate with them as fellow citizens, and thus fulfill one's own nature as a social being. Given the centrality of self-direction to self-perfection, then, respect for the rights of self-ownership turns out to be required for the successful pursuit of the moral life.

Other libertarian theorists take other aspects of the moral life and of human nature, understood in more or less Aristotelian terms, to call forth a distinctly libertarian account of rights. Ayn Rand, for instance, argued that the reality of natural rights, and in particular the possibility of forming rights to the resources one needs in order to live, is a precondition for the very survival of man as a rational animal (1964). (Nozick, incidentally, rejected this specifically Randian approach to defending natural rights, though Den Uyl and Rasmussen have challenged his objections. See the essays by Nozick, Den Uyl and Rasmussen in Paul 1981.) Murray Rothbard and Hans-Hermann Hoppe argue that the right of self-ownership is presupposed in the very use of one's body to act within the world, and in particular in the use of one's rational faculties and body parts (e.g. one's mouth) in argumentation, so that one cannot so much as *try* to argue against self-ownership without falling into a pragmatic self-contradiction (Rothbard 1998, xxxiv). Loren Lomasky (whose position is not precisely an Aristotelian one though it shares a certain family resemblance to such an approach) focuses on the fact that human beings are "project pursuers," who for the successful execution of their often radically diverse projects require the sort of autonomy guaranteed by libertarian rights (Lomasky 1987; see also Mack 1995 for a similar view). All these accounts, however, have in common the notion that the existence of the rights of self-ownership follows from deeper moral facts that are themselves determined by objective human nature.

Though Nozick himself does not give a specifically Aristotelian defense of his position, there are aspects of his work that suggest that such a defense harmonizes well with it. Nozick indicates that the notion that a human being has, by nature, the sorts of rights we've been discussing, has something to do with the fact that he is:

> a being able to formulate long-term plans for its life, able to consider and decide on the basis of abstract principles or considerations it formulates to itself and hence not merely the plaything of immediate stimuli, a being that limits its own behavior in accordance with some principles or picture it has of what an appropriate life is for itself and others, and so on... [and has] the ability to regulate and guide its life in accordance with some overall conception it chooses to accept. (1974, 49)

This set of facts about human beings is, Nozick says, in turn "connected with that elusive and difficult notion: the meaning of life. A person's shaping his life in accordance with some overall plan is his way of giving meaning to his life; only a being with the capacity to shape his life can have or strive for meaningful life" (50).

Nozick's view, then, appears to be that the possibility of a meaningful human life presupposes that an individual be able to decide upon an overall vision of how life should be lived and to act in accordance with that vision – to develop a certain kind of character, and, as Lomasky would put it, to pursue his own individual projects. If the Aristotelian is right, an analysis of the nature of this innate capacity and need for human beings to formulate their own plans of life will lead us to acknowledge mastery of the virtues as a necessary precondition for the successful formulation and execution of these plans. In any case, an individual's being able to live in accordance with such a vision presupposes, for Nozick, that his rights as a self-owner be respected.

That our rights as self-owners must be respected if we are to flourish is perhaps also implied by Nozick's example of "the experience machine" (1974, 42-45) (though Nozick himself does not explicitly draw the connection). Suppose you could be hooked up for life to a machine that would continuously feed into your brain any sequence of experiences you wanted it to – a "virtual reality" machine (as we'd call it today) of the sort featured in science-fiction films like *The Matrix* and *Vanilla Sky*, which would, if you so desired, guarantee a life of perpetual bliss (even causing you to forget that it's all just an illusion, if that's what you request). Would you go through with it? Nozick says that most of us would not. Pleasant experiences are simply not all that matter to us: We want to have *control* over our lives and not be the slaves of even a benign master (or machine) who dictates those lives for us; and we want to have genuine contact with an *objective reality*, not live in a delusional world entirely of our own making. Arguably a respect for self-ownership best allows us to do these things. Only if we take on the personal responsibility that is the concomitant of self-ownership, rather than expecting (indeed forcing) others to pay the costs of our misfortunes and failures, can we have the dignity of being masters of our own fate. Only if we acknowledge the self-ownership rights of *others* can we respect them as independent beings having their *own* plans and needs, rather than treating them in solipsistic fashion as if they were mere characters in *our* life story or resources for the realization of *our* ends.

An example from another area of moral life may help to flesh out the intuition that perhaps lies behind Nozick's "experience machine"

51

scenario (though it is probably not the sort of example the rather unconservative Nozick would himself use). As the conservative philosopher Roger Scruton argues with respect to the particular kind of solipsistic fantasy world occupied by the consumer of pornography:

> [F]antasy replaces the real, resistant, objective world with a pliant surrogate. And it is important to see why this matters. Life in the actual world is difficult and embarrassing. Most of all, it is difficult and embarrassing in our confrontation with other people who, by their very existence, make demands that we may be unwilling to meet. It requires a great force, a desire that fixes upon an individual, and sees that individual as unique and irreplaceable, if people are to make the sacrifices upon which the community depends for its longevity. It is far easier to take refuge in surrogates, which neither embarrass us nor resist our cravings. The habit grows of creating a compliant world of desire, in which the erotic force is dissipated and the needs of love denied. (2000, 63)

The viewer of pornography, Scruton argues, is attracted to it precisely because the people who occupy the fantasy are undemanding, ready to serve the viewer's whims without question and on his own terms. But real romantic relationships are not like that – they demand, if they are to succeed, that a person learn unselfishly to put his lover's needs, wishes, feelings and vulnerabilities on at least an equal footing with his own, that he move beyond the self and toward the other. Absorption in pornography makes it difficult to do this, as it ingrains a tendency to remove sex in the viewer's mind from the interpersonal contexts that concretely shape it in the real world, with all their complications and emotional attachments – to regard it in a self-gratifying way that objectifies the other person, rather than in self-giving and other-regarding terms. Hence the stress in traditional conservative thinking on the need for flourishing human beings to cultivate the virtue of chastity – to confine sexual passion to the context of total commitment to another human being in marriage.

Similarly, human beings need, if they are to flourish in their other (and usually less intimate!) relationships to other human beings to learn to regard those others as subjects and not objects, as fellow rational beings with their *own* needs and purposes, not selfishly and narcissistically as if they were figments of our own imaginations who exist and have significance only to the extent that they fulfill our *own* needs. Respecting another's self-ownership is a mark of moral maturity, reflecting one's recognition that that other person does not exist for *you*, to cater to *your* needs at *your* will – he is not your creation but an objective reality in his own right, and thus cannot be used by you against his will as a resource. The socialist or liberal egalitarian – who insists, in effect, that *others'* efforts and resources be directed or redistributed to fulfill his *own* needs and desires – would, on this view, be analogous to the occupant of Nozick's "experience machine" world or like the onanist of Scruton's pornography example, childishly demanding that the world be re-made to conform to his will. It is he, rather than the Nozickian libertarian, who is thus more plausibly accused of "selfishness." Respect for self-ownership is in fact profoundly *un*selfish – a necessary condition for dealing with other people in a manner that respects their independence and dignity, making possible the kind of human community that our nature as social beings requires us to work for.

The burden of proof

These thoughts require development, of course, if they are to count as a fully adequate account of how self-ownership may follow from an Aristotelian conception of the moral life. Such development would, however, take us far beyond the limits of Nozick's own position. In any case, as we've seen, such development is not required to provide Nozick's libertarianism with a powerful justification – the thesis of self-ownership is plausible enough by itself to do that. But we can end this long chapter – necessarily long given how crucial individual rights are to Nozick's project – by noting that even if that thesis were entirely lacking in justification, it is difficult to see why this would be especially problematic for Nozick. For why should we assume that it is *he* who has to justify the thesis? Why not assume instead that it is Nozick's *opponent* who must justify his *rejection* of it?

The burden of proof, I want to suggest, does in fact clearly lie with the opponent, and not with Nozick. For there are really only three possibilities: Either you own yourself, or other people do, or no one does. The last seems plainly false: Are we really to believe that *no one* owns your hand or your heart? Not even *you* – which would entail that *you* have no more of an entitlement to them than *I* do? But then if *someone* really does own them, it isn't just *obvious* who it is, namely you? They're attached to *you*, after all, and not to anyone else; indeed, your body and its parts seem *to be* you, or at least are partially *constitutive* of you. Are we expected to believe instead that someone else at least *partially* owns your hand or heart or other body parts, then? *Which* parts exactly, and on what terms? Do you own the fingers of your hand, but not the thumb? Or do you *co*-own them all – in which case, do you require someone's *permission* if you want to use them, or can you use them only on Thursdays and Sundays, say? And *who* exactly are the true owners or co-owners if not you? Your family? Friends? The government? (City, state, or federal?) And what exactly gives *them* ownership and not *you*? Are we really expected to believe that there is a serious problem in justifying your claim to use your body and labor as you wish, but no problem in justifying the *government's* claim to use them as *it* wishes?! Why do non-libertarians demand justification of the thesis of self-ownership but not for, say, the thesis of community-ownership or the thesis of state-ownership?

(Of course, someone might respond that *God* owns us, so that we cannot own ourselves – though presumably most of Nozick's socialist and liberal critics wouldn't say this. But self-ownership is no more inconsistent with belief in God than private property is. In both cases, we can suppose that God owns everything but allows *us* to act as stewards of what He owns, and holds us to account for how we use it. God owns the land your farm is on, say, but allows you to hold that land as your private property and forbids others from stealing it, or anything else, from you. Similarly, God owns *you*, but allows you to hold yourself as private property, and forbids others from stealing *that* property from you. On this view, "self-stewardship" would perhaps be a more appropriate term than self-ownership.)

The notion that anyone else has a rightful claim, enforceable by law, over your body, its parts, or your abilities, talents, and labor thus seems itself entirely undefended, and indeed indefensible. At any rate, the assumption that you are the owner of these things seems the obvious default position to take. The thesis of self-ownership has a presumption in its favor; it is "innocent until proven guilty." But then, so is the libertarianism that Nozick says follows from it. It is not *Nozick* who needs to "provide foundations" for or justify his libertarianism, then – it is his *critics* who need to justify themselves.

Is this too quick, however? After all, even if Nozick is right about *self*-ownership, does this really justify the strong private property rights – rights in things *other* than oneself – that he endorses? And if it does, then is Nozick perhaps not radical *enough* – wouldn't the taxation required to fund the minimal state be as immoral as the taxation that goes to fund social security and welfare programs, leaving anarchism rather than minarchism as the only *truly* libertarian position? The next two chapters deal with these questions, in reverse order.

4

From Anarchy to the Minimal State

The anarchist challenge

It is only to be expected that Nozick would face heavy criticism from the Left, on the part of those who insist on a more expansive government than the minimal state. But Nozick also faces a challenge on his Right, from those who argue that even minimal government is too much government. Individual rights to life, liberty, and property in fact entail that *no state whatsoever* can be justified – so argues the individualist anarchist or "anarcho-capitalist."

Some might find it odd to describe anarchism as a "right-wing" position. Haven't anarchist thinkers like Proudhon, Bakunin, Kropotkin, and Noam Chomsky been, in good Leftist fashion, harsh critics of capitalism and private property? Indeed, isn't Proudhon's "Property is theft!" the quintessential anarchist battle cry? But such left-wing anarchism is a muddle, in the view of anarcho-capitalists. "Theft," of course, just *means* the taking of someone's *property* without his consent – to criticize property *itself* as theft is thus simply incoherent. It is also futile, given that the institution of private property is universal and clearly reflects something deep in human nature (having as its biological ancestor the territoriality exhibited by the lower animals), and given that the economic incentives upon which material prosperity depends require it. Above all, the rejection of

55

private property is dangerously contrary to the individual freedom the left-wing anarchist claims to champion: A purportedly "anarchist" community that claims, a la socialism, "collective ownership" of all property has no less absolute power over the individual than does a totalitarian state.

Left-wing anarchism thus is, in the eyes of right-wing anarchists like Murray Rothbard and David Friedman, a quasi-statist sham. Private property is not theft – it is *liberty*, and any infringements on one's property are thus infringements on his liberty. It is "Taxation is theft!" that must serve as the watchword of the true anarchist, and the realization of unfettered laissez faire capitalism in *all* areas of political life – the *abolition* of the state through the *total privatization* of the functions of the state – that must be his program. In particular, the law enforcement functions that Nozick claims are within the legitimate domain of the minimal state can and should be handled not by government but by private firms voluntarily retained by individuals trading in the free market.

Why the anarcho-capitalist holds that this is morally required is perhaps not mysterious, being just an extension of Nozick's critique of the redistributive and paternalistic activities of the welfare state: If it is immoral for the state to force me to help others or to do what it thinks is for my own good, isn't it *also* immoral for it to force me to pay *it* for my own or another's protection? What if I would rather protect *myself*, or hire someone else to protect me, rather than pay the government, through taxes, to provide protection through its police and courts of law? It is *my* life, liberty, and property that are at stake, and thus surely only *I* have a right to decide how best to protect them.

It might seem less clear why the anarcho-capitalist should think this is *realistic* or even *possible*. Yet libertarian anarchist thinkers have in fact developed detailed and fascinating models of how the law enforcement functions now performed by police and courts of law could be performed instead, and performed more efficiently, by private protection agencies, arbitration firms, and the like (Barnett 1998; Benson 1990; Friedman 1989; Rothbard 1978). Many of the resulting institutions would *parallel* existing governmental ones – private homeowners associations and the security firms they employ could evolve into sizable quasi-"city governments," the larger scale protection agencies clusters of cities employ to defend themselves might develop into quasi-"federal governments," etc. – but such bodies would be fairly fluid, for participation in them would be entirely voluntary and contractual, with firms constantly having to compete with one another to retain the business of individuals and associations.

Law and order in the state of nature

Nozick himself clearly sympathizes with the moral and practical claims made for such an anarcho-capitalist model of society. But, far from regarding this model as a refutation of his position, he argues that the minimal state in fact *follows* from it. His strategy is to show that a minimal state would inevitably arise, as a result of an "invisible hand" process and in a way that violates no one's rights, out of a state of anarchy. Since such a state is the practical and moral consequence of the anarchist's own commitments, he can thus have no objection to it.

The dominant protective association

Suppose there is no state – people live in an anarchic society, a "state of nature," as political philosophers have traditionally described it. Being self-owners, individuals have rights, and they will want to protect these rights against infringements by other individuals. They could do this on their own – standing guard over their property, making sure to stay well-armed while going about their daily business, and so forth – but this is inconvenient and time consuming, and there are lots of other things they'd rather be doing. Inevitably, individuals will band together to form mutual protection societies, agreeing to "watch each other's backs" as it were, perhaps taking turns monitoring everyone's property for extended periods of time. Eventually, some will get the idea that there is money to be made in protective services, and will devote themselves full-time to running protective agencies, private firms providing protection services to subscribers for a fee.

Different such firms will compete with one another for customers. Larger and more resourceful firms will, because they can provide better protection at a cheaper price, tend to attract more subscribers. And given that so much is at stake – one's property, liberty, indeed one's very life – this is one market where bigger will be seen necessarily to mean better, and most individuals will flock to the most powerful agency. Furthermore, there will, unavoidably, be conflicts between the clients of different firms. Sometimes, of course, this will be because one party is simply and clearly in the wrong. But often both parties to a dispute will be well-meaning: Fred may genuinely believe, on the basis of good evidence, that Bob has stolen his property, while Bob is in fact innocent and has been framed. Fred will reasonably want his protection agency to arrest and punish Bob, while Bob will reasonably want *his* agency to protect him against false arrest and undeserved punishment. How will their respective agencies settle this dispute? They *could* simply go to war – but battle is costly, and will become increasingly frequent if firms are not careful to determine in the first place whether or not their clients are in fact innocent. It will thus pay for agencies to agree to settle disputes between clients by appealing to a neutral third party – a private arbitration firm, say, which numerous firms may retain – as well as to require their clients to sign over all rights to finding and punishing the guilty to the agencies themselves, so that unnecessary disputes between agencies are not caused by some individual client's ill-considered vigilante behavior. There will thus be a tendency within the state of nature toward a kind of natural monopoly where protection services are concerned – toward a single dominant agency or a single confederation of agencies united by commitment to common arbitration procedures (Nozick 1974, 15-17).

The ultra-minimal state

So far the society we're describing is still an anarchist one – there is no state, though there is an entity that has many of the state's features, i.e. the dominant protective association. But this entity will, Nozick argues, inevitably take on the features of a state, and do so in a way that is entirely morally legitimate. How so? Consider that, however large the dominant agency, there will still be those who do not subscribe to it – independents who seek to go it alone or to stick with smaller firms which refuse to deal with the dominant agency. How will the dominant agency deal with disputes between its clients and these independents? Will it simply allow them to arrest, try, and punish its clients on their own – perhaps using procedures that are unreliable, or exacting extreme and unjust punishments on those found guilty? Nozick argues that it cannot and will not. The dominant agency has been hired to protect its clients' rights – it cannot allow those rights to be threatened by hotheads who are not careful enough in determining guilt, or who are prone to excessive punishments. It will thus have to announce a general policy of forbidding independents and rival agencies from applying procedures and punishments that it has not itself approved. The dominant agency, then, can and must legitimately engage in *prohibition* of activities that put its clients' rights at risk. But in prohibiting such risky behavior and requiring its own clients to cede to it their rights to punish offenders – in setting itself up, that is, as the sole authorizer of legitimate violence – the dominant agency has taken on one of the defining features of a state. It has become what Nozick calls an "ultra-minimal state" (1974, 26).

Prohibition and compensation

This ultra-minimal state acts justly in prohibiting independents

58

from engaging in behavior that puts its own clients at risk. But those independents do, after all, still have a right to protect their *own* rights – something the ultra-minimal state has now forbidden them to do. So the ultra-minimal state cannot legitimately rest with prohibition of their self-protection. It must (*morally* must) provide *compensation* for this prohibition. And this means that the ultra-minimal state must *itself* provide these independents with protective services. It may charge an independent for providing these services to him, but only an amount the independent would have had to spend anyway in protecting himself – any costs over that amount must be borne by the ultra-minimal state, and thus, by extension, by the ultra-minimal state's clients (110-113).

With this turn of events, however, the ultra-minimal state has taken on a further feature of a full-blown state, in that it provides protection for everyone in the geographical area it occupies, and charges them for that protection. It thus engages in a kind of taxation – but *this* taxation (and *only* this taxation) does not amount to theft. Its original clients pay *voluntarily* to retain its services, after all; and though their payments may end up partially subsidizing the protection of the independents, this too is simply part of the package they voluntarily agreed to in signing up with the agency, rather than being a kind of coerced aid to the needy in the form of welfare. The independents are also at least partially charged for protection, but only an amount they would have paid anyway to protect themselves, and only insofar as they insist on engaging in behavior that potentially puts *others'* rights at risk. So the ultra-minimal state, in providing compensation for prohibited risky activity, violates no one's rights. But in doing so, it has in effect moved beyond being an *ultra*-minimal state to being a full *minimal* state, full stop. Our original anarchist community has, then, developed inexorably and in an entirely morally legitimate manner into a minimal state. There thus can be no principled objection on the anarchist's part to Nozick's minimal state. For such a state practically and morally *has* to arise out of anarchy itself.

The "immaculate conception" of the state

The point of Nozick's argument is to show that the minimal state must be judged morally acceptable *even by the anarchist's own strict standards* – that it is, contrary to appearances and in Rothbard's phrase, "immaculately conceived" (Rothbard 1998, 232). But critics have alleged that the argument in fact fails even by *Nozick's* own standards. Consider his claim that the dominant protective association can legitimately prohibit activity risky to its clients under the condition that it compensate those disadvantaged by the prohibition. This, by Nozick's own admission, seems to open the door to a notion of "procedural rights" – rights, that is, to be treated by the legal system according to certain (reliable) procedures (Nozick 1974, 96). Yet wouldn't a procedural right be a kind of *positive* right – a right against others that they provide one with certain things? And wouldn't this conflict with the notion that the rights of self-ownership are entirely *negative* (Rothbard 1998, 250)? Furthermore, doesn't the principle of prohibition of risky activity amount to an acknowledgement that rights are, after all, not compatible – that there can be conflicts of rights, between e.g. my right to punish those I believe have violated my rights, and your right not to be unjustly punished (Wolff 1991, 66)? And doesn't that principle also open the door to a *more*-than-minimal state, a government that prohibits just *any* behavior it deems a "risk" to the rights of others (Rothbard 1998, 239)?

Fortunately for Nozick, all these questions can be answered in the negative, for the appearance of inconsistency in his position is illusory. Your "procedural right" to be treated a certain way is, I think, best seen as following, not directly from your rights of self-ownership, but indirectly, from everyone else's *duty* to *respect* your rights of self-ownership. It is because I have a duty not to violate your rights that I have a duty to make sure that I do not punish you unjustly. It is in *that* sense that you have a procedural "right" – it isn't some positive right to part of my wealth or labor, but a corollary of your negative right not to be unjustly harmed; it doesn't involve a *positive* duty on my part to give you certain things, so much as a *negative* duty to make sure I don't unjustly deprive you of what's already justly yours. (True, I may have to *do* something to fulfill this duty – so that there is, in one sense, a "positive" obligation involved – but *all* negative rights entail *some* such "positive" actions under *some* circumstances, e.g. a duty on my part to exert the effort needed to swerve my car out of your way if I see you in the street ahead of me. But this is obviously a very different kind of thing from an alleged positive obligation to provide you with an education, health care, welfare, etc. *That* sort of obligation does *not* follow from any negative right of yours.)

Nor is there, in the relevant sense, any conflict of rights in Nozick's account. The positive rights championed by socialists and liberals clash *in principle* with negative rights and with each other. Even under the best possible circumstances, your purported right to an education funded by me conflicts with my negative right to my income and with some *other* person's purported positive right to the same part of my income (to fund his health insurance or retirement plan, say).

But negative rights do *not* clash in principle. If we were omniscient, and just *knew* who was guilty and who was innocent, there would be no need for the minimal state to prohibit risky rights-enforcing activity and no need for talk of "procedural rights" at all. These needs follow, not from any intrinsic feature of the principle of self-ownership, but rather from the contingent circumstances that affect our *application* of that principle. And *any* moral principle is going to be so affected – this isn't a special problem for Nozick's position. No moral theory can reasonably be expected to enable us to avoid *all* conflicts *in practice*, for this is simply impossible given the limitations on human knowledge. It *is* reasonable to expect that it be able to avoid conflicts *in principle* however – and Nozick's position, unlike that of positive rights advocates, does avoid such conflicts.

That the principle of prohibition of risky behavior is a requirement *only* given such conditions as our ignorance in certain circumstances of how best to guarantee respect for others' rights of self-ownership, also helps us see why Nozick's view does not open the floodgates to government's prohibiting whatever it wishes to. Where ignorance and the like are not factors, there is no legitimate case for prohibition. There is no problem, for instance, in knowing whether or not my chewing tobacco puts *you* at risk, whatever risk it poses to *me* – we have good reason to believe that it does not affect you at all. The state could thus not legitimately appeal to the principle of prohibition of behavior risky to others to justify outlawing tobacco chewing.

But what about *smoking* tobacco – especially given the (largely bogus – see Sullum 1998) allegations so often made these days about the dangers of "second-hand smoke"? Wouldn't Nozick's principle allow the state, in a most unlibertarian fashion, to outlaw your smoking in your own back yard, since a bit of smoke might waft over my fence and irritate my sensitive nostrils? But we must keep in mind that the whole *point* of the principle of prohibiting risky activity is to safeguard self-ownership and the liberties that follow from it. It is in essence a *prudential* and second-order principle, helping us to fulfill the *absolute*, first-order duties entailed by respect for self-ownership, under conditions of ignorance. That entails that we must *strive* to avoid applying the principle in a way that effectively stifles self-ownership rights. The burden of proof must *always* be on the person proposing a prohibition to show that it is justified, *not* on the person who opposes a prohibition. It is one thing for me to justify my shooting of the hapless deaf vagrant I find had wandered into my house one night on the grounds that I feared he was an intruder intent on harming me and my family, and that he did not respond to my warnings; it is another thing

61

altogether to claim that one can legitimately take pot shots at passing motorists because one of them *could* after all be a murderer. Similarly, while a government that prohibits private enforcement of justice acts on good prudential grounds, justified by its need to protect the rights of the innocent, one that was constantly looking for loopholes via which it could prohibit various *other* activities would be manifestly unjust. Of course, where exactly to "draw the line" will not always be obvious; but then, *no* moral principle is easy to apply in every single case, and given the human condition, it is unreasonable to expect otherwise. Given the thesis of self-ownership, however, it is also unreasonable to give the benefit of the doubt to anyone but the opponent of a prohibition. And it is surely unreasonable to suggest that there are any grounds to believe that smoking in one's back yard poses anything like a justification for rousing the libertarian "nightwatchman" state from its slumber, when there is such a strong presumption against doing so.

Furthermore, we must not forget that the principle of prohibition always gets applied in concert with the principle of *compensation* – and the latter principle serves as a serious deterrent to anyone looking to prohibit activities willy-nilly. Your anti-smoking activist neighbor might think it a neat idea to try to get the state to ban your smoking in your backyard if he thinks this will affect only you; he will, however, think twice if he has to *compensate* you (either directly or through his taxes) for so inconveniencing you. Busybodies can generally be kept at bay when *they*, and not just the targets of their activism, have to bear the costs of their frenzy for banning things they claim threaten them.

Now some anarchist critics of Nozick (e.g. Rothbard 1998, 238) seek to side-step the messiness that is unavoidable in applying to everyday life Nozick's principles of prohibition and compensation (or *any* moral principle, for that matter) by simply denying that *any* behavior risky to others can *ever* legitimately be prohibited. For until rights are *actually* violated, and not merely put at risk, no injustice has been done and there are thus no grounds for interference with another's behavior. But the implausibility of this view should be obvious. If my neighbor with Parkinson's disease likes to juggle vials of nitroglycerin by the side of the fence separating our homes, must I do nothing until he finally slips up one day and blows up himself, his property, and *my* property too? If instead he enjoys tinkering with old radioactive bomb casings out in the garage, should I nevertheless leave him be and console myself with the thought that if some radiation makes its way over to my house, I might live long enough to file a liability suit against him? And what if he likes making *bombs* with those casings? (And wears an Osama bin Laden T-shirt?) Or suppose the danger to my property is even more immediate. What if I see your ladder falling from the side of your house and toward the windshield of my new Ferrari? Can I throw a rock at the ladder to knock it out of the way, thus slightly damaging it? Or, mindful of your property rights and of the fact that my rights haven't *yet* been violated, must I simply let it fall, hoping against hope that you'll appear with a lasso to catch it at the last moment?

If all this seems absurd, consider that it would also seem to follow from the Rothbard view that I cannot even defend myself against an apparent direct intentional assault. After all, until you *actually* plunge the knife into me, you haven't really violated my rights. And who knows, maybe you don't *really* mean to in the first place – maybe you're just an eccentric prankster with excellent balance, and will stop the knife before it gets within a hair's breadth of my shirt. Better wait for the knife to go in before I defend myself, lest my "self-defense" really turn out *itself* to be an assault, and you sue me for being unable to take a joke. But even Rothbard does not go this far. "[T]he threat to commit aggressive violence is itself aggression," he says, and may justly be prohibited (1998, 248, n. 43). Yet if it is legitimate to prohibit the mere *threat* of a rights violation, and not merely the violation itself, why is it not also legitimate to prohibit actions that *risk* the violation of another's rights?

The *reason* it is legitimate to prohibit threats, Rothbard says, is simply that my having a right to something just *entails* a right to defend it against threats to it and/or to hire others to do so (77), at least if those threats are "palpable, immediate, and direct" (78). But clearly, that reason would *also* make it legitimate to prohibit the risk of rights violations. Your threatening me with the knife is no *more* "palpable, immediate, and direct" a danger than your juggling nitroglycerin. More to the point, it is no more palpable, immediate, and direct than your threatening me with false arrest and unmerited punishment. Thus the minimal state, which by hypothesis on Nozick's analysis I've hired to protect me, has a right to defend me against this threat. "But you might *really be* guilty and thus *merit* the punishment!", the Rothbardian replies. But the minimal state doesn't *know* that. So shouldn't it insist on *finding out* before it lets me be punished? Doesn't respect for the rights of self-ownership *morally require* it to do so?

Rothbard also objects that Nozick's argument is useless if applied to any state other than one that *actually arose* in the manner he describes, which would obviously not be true of any existing government (1998, 232). So any existing government would still be illegitimate *even if* it became minimal, and the most Nozick's argument shows is that some future, *post*-anarchy minimal state could be legitimate. But as Jonathan Wolff has noted, the hypothetical historical scenario Nozick describes is not really essential to his argument, but just a way of clearly illustrating its main point (1991, 52). And that point is, I think, that given the principles of prohibition of risk and compensation (and the circumstances of imperfect human knowledge, etc. these principles are meant to deal with), *any* individual, group of individuals, or firm that seeks to protect rights *inevitably will* and *morally must* claim minimal-state-like powers. This is so even if we grant, as Nozick as much as the anarchist would, the right to "opt out" or *secede* from the state and its activities (Nozick 1974, 110, 113) – the "right to ignore the state," as Herbert Spencer called it (Spencer 1995, chapter 19). The minimal state *doesn't* forbid independents or groups of independents from refusing its protection and setting up their own procedures; it's just that, if they insist on doing so, they will still not be allowed to take action against the minimal state's *own* clients, and that given the circumstances of human life that apply even within their own domains, they will in effect become "miniature minimal states" themselves, states within the borders of the minimal state. (The obvious *inconvenience* of this, and not coercion, is what will lead most of them to give in and join the minimal state.) So even if anarchy were established today, minimal states would in effect come into existence *immediately* (and no doubt start merging into larger minimal states).

Given this fact, it seems pointless to insist on abolishing all existing states before setting up a minimal one. Better to try to pare down states that do exist to acceptable libertarian levels. This would be what the prudence and caution that wisdom requires of us in applying *any* moral principle in the context of the unavoidable untidiness inherent in the human condition would entail in any case.

That rather conservative thought leads us to another one. If, as many libertarians do, we accept a Hayekian analysis of institutions in terms of cultural evolution (as described in chapter 2), we will be led to wonder whether a state of some sort is not *inevitable* – surely it is a most robust survivor the cultural-evolutionary process, there being virtually no society in which a state has not existed. But Hayekian analysis also shows the superiority of market-based institutions and the principles of self-ownership and private property they rest on, principles which when consistently applied lead to libertarianism. Surely it is a virtue of Nozick's position that it allows us to harmonize these cultural-evolutionary facts, and thus leads to the same result that a Hayekian approach to justifying libertarianism does: At *least* a libertarian state is justified, but at *most* a libertarian state is justified.

5

Distributive Justice and Private Property

The Entitlement Theory of Justice

Most of those who object to the minimal state want, not less government than Nozick does, but more. Their complaint is that a libertarian state will inevitably fail to guarantee *distributive justice*, i.e. a just distribution of wealth and income among the members of society. A more-than-minimal state is required, in their view, to provide for this, by *re*distributing, according to some moral criterion, the wealth produced by and divided unequally and amorally within a capitalist economy. Nozick, unsurprisingly, disagrees. He argues that a correct account of distributive justice will show that justice does *not* require *any* particular distribution, much less a redistribution, of wealth; and that in fact, justice *forbids* the redistribution of wealth. Such an account is represented by Nozick's "entitlement theory" of justice.

The first thing to note about talk of distributive justice, Nozick says, is how misleading it is. It makes it sound as if there is some central authority who determines who will get what and "distributes" wealth accordingly – as if some government bureaucrat, say, decided to give Bill Gates 40 billion dollars, you 40 thousand, and the guy on skid row 40 cents, and has failed to dole out the shares fairly. It also makes it sound as if this wealth simply appeared from nowhere waiting to be "distributed" (Nozick 1974, 160) or fell from the sky like "manna from heaven" (198). But of course, the real world doesn't work like that. Wealth comes into existence only because individual human beings *create* it by exercising their powers over natural resources; and it comes to be "distributed" only as a consequence of innumerable scattered transactions between individuals, undirected by any central authority:

> [W]e are not in the position of children who have been given portions of pie by someone who now makes last minute adjustments to rectify careless cutting. There is no *central* distribution, no person or group entitled to control all the resources, jointly deciding how they are to be doled out. What each person gets, he gets from others who give to him in exchange for something, or as a gift. In a free society, diverse persons control different resources, and new holdings arise out of the voluntary exchanges and actions of persons. There is no more a distributing or distribution of shares than there is a distributing of mates in a society in which persons choose whom they shall marry. The total result is the product of many individual decisions which the different individuals involved are entitled to make. (1974, 149-150)

F.A. Hayek concluded from this that the very concept of "'social' or distributive justice" is incoherent or meaningless (Hayek 1976; Feser 1997; Feser 1998). For talk of justice or injustice presupposes some *agent* who consciously and with foresight acts so as to bring about a particular result; and there is no such agent in a capitalist economy, where the *overall* distribution of wealth results, not from anyone's decision, but through blind and impersonal market processes. The distribution of wealth in a free market society is thus *neither* just *nor* unjust; it just *is*. Nozick, though he seems to sympathize with such a view, nevertheless declines to reject *all* talk of distributive justice. His aim is rather to show that even if there is such a thing as distributive justice, it really favors his own libertarian position rather than the redistributive approach of his critics.

The three principles of justice in holdings

Nozick does not attempt to offer a fully worked out theory of justice, one that answers every question we might have about justice in people's holdings. He offers only a sketch, but a sketch is all he needs in order to answer his redistributionist critics. A complete theory, Nozick says, would elaborate three principles (1974, 150-153):

1. The principle of justice in acquisition: This principle would spell out the conditions under which one could justly come to appropriate as his own property some part of the natural world that had previously been unowned. One such principle that has greatly influenced libertarian theory is provided by John Locke's famous theory of property: An individual, being a self-owner, owns his labor; and by "mixing his labor" with some unowned part of the natural world (e.g. by whittling a piece of driftwood into a spear) he thereby comes to own *it* (Locke 1967; Nozick 1974, 174-182). Locke's idea seems to be that by inextricably mixing something you own with some object that no one else already owns, you thereby come to own that object. There is a qualification, however: You must leave "enough and as good" for others to acquire for themselves (e.g. enough driftwood of as good quality as the driftwood you've whittled). This is what has come to be known as the "Lockean Proviso" on just acquisition, and violations of this proviso would count as violations of the principle of justice in acquisition itself. The extent to which Nozick accepts all the details of Locke's theory is, as we'll see, not entirely clear; but the theory does provide a prima facie plausible account of how unowned resources might justly come to be transformed into private holdings.

2. The principle of justice in transfer: This principle would explain how one might come justly to acquire a holding previously held by some other person – how one person's property can rightfully become another's. Though Nozick does not spell this principle out in detail, it is clear that, as Jonathan Wolff notes, "the essential core of Nozick's principle of justice in transfer is that a transfer is just if and only if it is voluntary" (Wolff 1991, 78). If you justly own some holding, and you freely exchange it with someone else for some holding of his or freely give it away as a gift, then that transfer is just. Nothing more and nothing less is needed – how *could* any more be required, given that it was *your* property in the first place, and that you *agreed* to give it up? Violation of this principle would involve theft or fraud – taking someone's property without his consent, or exchanging something for it under false pretenses (e.g. misrepresenting the condition of the holding you're giving in exchange, or transferring stolen property).

3. The principle of justice in rectification: This principle would detail how past violations of the principles of justice in acquisition and transfer are to be corrected – how injustices suffered by individuals here and now due to theft or fraud committed against their ancestors, for example, or due to past violations of the Lockean Proviso, are to be made right.

However these three principles are to be spelled out in detail, they will in Nozick's view exhaust the principles that a theory of justice in holdings needs to provide. And together they give the necessary and sufficient conditions under which an individual is *entitled* to the holdings he possesses: Simply put, a person is fully entitled to (i.e. he has a *right* to) any holding that he acquires either in accordance with the principle of justice in acquisition, or in accordance with the principle of justice in transfer (from someone else who was himself entitled to that holding) (1974, 151). And this in turn gives us all the criterion we need for a "just distribution" of wealth: "The complete principle of distributive justice would say simply that a distribution is just if everyone is entitled to the holdings they possess under the distribution," with "entitled" understood in the manner just outlined (151). This, in a nutshell, is Nozick's entitlement theory of justice.

Classification of theories of distributive justice

The entitlement theory is an extremely simple theory, and may at first glance even seem rather obvious and trivial – so much so that it might be hard to see what all the fuss is about. But its implications are radical, as can be seen by Nozick's comparison of his theory with other theories of distributive justice.

There are, according to Nozick, two broad categories into which theories of justice fall: *end-result* (or *end-state*) theories on the one hand, and *historical* theories on the other (1974, 153-155). An end-result theory holds that the justice or injustice of a particular distribution of wealth depends only on its *structure*. For example, a utilitarian who held that a just distribution of wealth was one that promoted the greatest happiness of the greatest number would be promoting an end-result conception, as would an egalitarian who insisted that a distribution is just only if it is equal. In both cases, the idea is that *how* the distribution came about is irrelevant – what matters is only the end result of the distribution (happiness, or equality). Historical theories, by contrast, hold that *how* the distribution came about – its historical background – *is* important, even crucial: We can't look just at who has what; we need to look also at *how they got it*, and whether they got it in a way that satisfies certain moral criteria.

Historical theories themselves can be further divided into two subcategories, viz. *patterned* and *unpatterned* (1974, 155-160). A patterned historical theory of justice holds that the specific historical circumstances underlying a just distribution involve that distribution's fitting a certain pattern. For instance, such a theory might hold that a just distribution is one in which those who *labored* the most get the most, or in which those who *need* the most get the most, or in which those who *merit* or morally deserve the most get the most. An unpatterned historical theory, by contrast, holds that such patterns are irrelevant to the justice of a distribution.

Nozick's entitlement theory is historical rather than end-result oriented, and unpatterned rather than patterned. On his view, whether a distribution of wealth has a certain structure or fits a certain pattern is *irrelevant* to it's being just or unjust; all that matters is whether people got what they have in accordance with the principles of justice in acquisition and transfer. If not, then the distribution as a whole is unjust (though the holdings of particular individuals may still be just); and the principle of justice in rectification must then be applied in order to make things right. But if so, then the overall distribution *is* just – *regardless* of whether it is equal or unequal, promotes happiness or not, or rewards those who labor, need, or merit the most. Of course, we may value equality in wealth, or happiness, or fulfilling people's needs, or rewarding hard work or merit; and we might seek to encourage people voluntarily to promote these values. This is all well and good; but it has nothing to do with whether or not a distribution of wealth as a whole is just or not. If everyone has what he has because he justly acquired it from the unowned portion of the natural world, or because he was given it as a gift or bought or traded for it fair and square, then everyone's holdings are just – *period*. That some people have less than others, that some work hard without much financial result, that some morally deserving people are poor while other, immoral people make the big money, and so forth, may be *regrettable*, but as long as everyone's holdings are a result of voluntary transactions, it is *not* unjust. That I've been unable to get my business off the ground, or that people would rather pay to listen to bad music or read *Playboy* than hear me deliver a scintillating philosophy lecture, does not mean that Bill Gates, Britney Spears, Hugh Hefner or anyone else, has done me wrong by succeeding where I failed. It does not entitle me to a portion of *their* incomes, much less to *your* income or the incomes of other taxpayers. To have a streak of bad luck is simply not the same thing as to suffer an injustice.

Calls to take from the rich and give to the poor so as to achieve a more "equitable" distribution of wealth, and maxims like Marx's famous "From each according to his ability, to each according to his need" are thus fundamentally misguided. For the attainment of "distributive justice" does not require that some central agency must do any actual *distributing*, whether according to need, labor, merit, or whatever; it doesn't call for such an agency to take "from" some people and give "to" certain other people so as to make the *overall* distribution come out a certain way. It requires *only* that the millions of scattered *individual transactions* made between *individual persons* within a society be made voluntarily. If one demands some pithy slogan with which to sum up the demands of distributive justice, then, it can only be this: "From each as they choose, to each as they are chosen" (160).

The "Wilt Chamberlain" argument

Nozick elucidates and defends the entitlement theory by appealing to a thought experiment involving Wilt Chamberlain, the famous basketball player (1974, 160-164). Suppose there is a society in which a certain distribution of wealth and income – call it D1 – prevails, and let it be any end-result or patterned distribution that an opponent of Nozick would insist upon. To keep things simple, let's imagine that D1 is an equal distribution of wealth (though the argument will come out the same whatever distribution we choose). Nozick's opponent will have to grant that D1 is a *just* distribution – after all, *he's* the one who decided on it. Now let's suppose further, that among the members of this society is Wilt Chamberlain. Chamberlain is popular, and many people want to see him play basketball. Imagine, however, that he insists on playing only if those who come to watch his games pay him an extra 25 cents, dropping a quarter in a special box at the gate before entering the sports arena. Some people will prefer to keep their money and will stay home. But others will happily part with their 25 cents in order to watch him play; and let's suppose that over the course of the season, 1 million of them do so.

What we have at the end of the season is thus a new distribution of wealth, D2; and this distribution breaks the original pattern, being unequal, since Chamberlain now has $250,000 more than anyone else has. So now we want to ask: Is Chamberlain entitled to his money? And is the new distribution D2 a *just* distribution? The answer, Nozick says, is obviously *yes*. For each individual in D1 was *entitled* to what he had, as Nozick's own critic, being the one who chose D1, must acknowledge; so no one can complain that the starting point was unjust. But neither can anyone complain that any of the steps from D1 to D2 were unjust. For some of the individuals in D1 *freely chose* to exchange some of their holdings with Chamberlain – *they* thus have no grounds for a complaint of injustice. The others didn't make this choice, but they thus *still have* the shares they had under D1 – so *they* have no grounds for a complaint either. But then *no one* has grounds for a complaint of injustice, either against Chamberlain or against D2 itself; and thus there *is* no injustice. "Whatever arises from a just situation by just steps is itself just," Nozick says (151); in particular, D2 is perfectly just, and Chamberlain has a right to his newly gained wealth.

This implies, though, that *all* end-result and patterned theories of distributive justice are *false*. For such theories hold that to be just, a distribution of wealth must fit a certain pattern. Yet the Chamberlain example clearly shows that a distribution can be just *without* fitting any particular pattern. D2 is perfectly just even though, unlike D1, it is not an equal distribution; so egalitarian theories of justice, which hold that only an equal distribution can be just, are just wrong. A similar result would follow if we imagined instead that D1 was a distribution according to need, labor, merit, or what have you. In each case, people freely choosing to pay Chamberlain 25 cents (even if he doesn't need it, or doesn't work as hard as others, or may not be morally exemplary) will break the favored pattern, and yet this won't result in an unjust distribution. So a just distribution does not require that those who need, work, or merit the most get the most. The Wilt Chamberlain argument shows, then, that criticisms of capitalist societies to the effect that "x% of the population own much more than x% of the wealth," or that there are people in them who work hard but deserve or need much more than they have, are without force. How equal or unequal an overall distribution of wealth is in a society or how well this or that individual does within it, *by itself* tells you *nothing whatsoever* about whether that society is just. That does not mean that we shouldn't care about whether people have enough to eat, etc.; it does mean, however, that as long as violations of the principles of acquisition and transfer aren't in question, such matters are *not* matters of justice (which might call for government action) but rather matters of charity (and thus properly taken care of only through private initiative).

Some have alleged that Nozick's argument begs the question in that it presupposes that those given shares under D1 are "entitled" to them in Nozick's strong sense of having an *absolute property right* in them – a presupposition that Nozick's opponent would, of course, reject (Kymlicka 1990, 103). But the argument assumes no such thing. It need assume, not that you can do *anything* you like with what you're given under D1, but only that you can freely do at least *something* with it. And surely no critic of Nozick is going to dispute *that* assumption – as Nozick asks, "what was it for if not to do something with?" (Nozick 1974, 161). But as long as individuals can do *something* with their shares, surely they can in principle do something that breaks the pattern, yet (because they did it voluntarily) without thereby creating an injustice.

Another objection suggests that not all transactions in a free market are plausibly regarded as truly "voluntary" or non-coercive; as Wolff argues, some people might agree to certain exchanges (e.g. of work for low wages) out of extreme need, and thus in a sense have no choice (1991, 83-84). Nozick's position is that an exchange is never truly involuntary unless it violates a person's rights (1974, 262), so that even if one makes an exchange out of desperation, he acts voluntarily so long as his rights weren't violated. Now Wolff recognizes this, but claims that if we accept Nozick's account of what counts as voluntary, the intuitive force of his argument is undermined. But in fact, even if one rejected Nozick's interpretation of "voluntary," the Chamberlain argument would not lose its force. For all Nozick needs for that argument to go through is the claim that *some* voluntary acts will lead to a D2 type distribution, and that claim is difficult to deny. Surely on *any* plausible account of voluntary action, libertarian or otherwise, an action as innocuous as choosing to pay 25 cents to watch Chamberlain play basketball is going to count as voluntary. But then the transition from D1 to D2 involves no coercion, and is thus not unjust.

Patterns vs. liberty

There is another lesson of the Wilt Chamberlain argument, namely that "liberty upsets patterns" (160), in that people's free choices to use their wealth as they see fit will eventually and inevitably destroy any pattern insisted upon by a non-entitlement theory of justice. And the corollary of this is that "no end-state principle or distributional patterned principle of justice can be continuously realized without continuous interference with people's lives" (163) and thus the destruction of individual liberty. To maintain an equal distribution, for example, would require preventing people, by force, from engaging in any transaction which might lead to inequality: "The socialist society would have to forbid capitalist acts between consenting adults" (163). The tyranny that has been such a prominent feature of actual socialist societies – in the old Soviet Union, China, Cuba, etc. – is just what we should expect from any attempt seriously to institute an end-state or patterned principle of distributive justice.

Some might find this objection to such principles rather overheated, and the alleged threat wildly exaggerated. For aren't the redistributive welfare states existing in capitalist societies motivated precisely by end-state or patterned theories of justice? Yet such societies cannot plausibly be regarded as tyrannical (Haworth 1994, 93). But notice that the advocates of these welfare states themselves never seem satisfied with the results their favored system has produced. In the United States, for example, the trillions of dollars spent on welfare programs since the 1960s, along with the institution of affirmative action programs and other government regulation of business intended to affect the overall distribution of wealth, have not radically increased equality or eliminated poverty. Indeed, what we have seen instead is the creation of a permanent "underclass," a *cycle* of poverty associated with a culture of illegitimacy, drug addiction, and crime that is passed along from generation to generation (Murray 1994). Welfare advocates conclude from this that *not enough* redistribution of wealth has taken place (apparently on the rather curious theory that if X isn't working, the remedy must be to try *more* of X). And in general, advocates of end-state or patterned principles typically complain that those principles are *not* sufficiently applied in capitalist welfare states – indeed, their complaint is often that such states are precisely still *capitalist* welfare states. So it will not do to point to capitalist societies as examples of societies in which such principles are applied in a non-tyrannical way, for the simple reason that they are typically *not* consistently applied in such societies in the first place.

And it's a good thing they are not, the libertarian would argue. For as implied above, the application of such principles typically only *exacerbates* the problems they are intended to solve. A *guarantee* of welfare benefits, for instance, in effect *subsidizes* the sort of irresponsible behavior that locks one and one's offspring into perpetual poverty. As noted in chapter 3, there is less motivation to look after a piece of property – including yourself – when someone *else* (the government) is paying the costs for damage to it. Moreover, the price paid for this transferal to others of the costs of one's misbehavior is *dependence* on those others, dependence, in this case, on the state – and thus the loss of one's full *liberty*. Such a loss of liberty is also suffered (though less dramatically) by the *middle* classes of a welfarist society. For those classes become dependent on state-run social security and health care programs which, because of the high taxes these entail, leave individuals with less money to save and invest for private retirement or health care options, and which also, given the distortions of the price mechanism and absence of market competition they embody (as discussed in chapter 2), are inevitably highly bureaucratized and inefficient, and chronically in danger of bankruptcy. This calls forth complaints from the population, which results in *further* government regulation of economic behavior (e.g. in the health care industry) and even higher taxation, which only brings about *further* distortions of the price mechanism, even *less* market competition, and a *further* decrease in the ability of individuals to pay for private alternatives – and thus yet greater dependency on the (ever increasingly deficient) services of the state. This results in turn in *yet further* government action, which only *further exacerbates* the problem, *ad infinitum.* The internal logic of government manipulation of the economic system in the interests of furthering some patterned principle of justice thus leads society toward ever-increasing control of the state over the life of the individual and ever increasing dependency of individuals on the state (Hayek 1944; Hayek 1976; Mises 1951).

The point isn't that this vicious cycle is absolutely inexorable; it *can* in principle be arrested and turned back, and to a limited extent *was* turned back in many Western democracies during the 1980's and 1990's under conservative governments. But this arresting of the cycle necessarily involved – as its critics on the Left complained – precisely an abandonment of the egalitarian redistributive principles that had got the cycle started in the first place. For a *serious* and *consistent* application of such principles *does* inevitably lead to a loss of liberty. Nor is this loss a loss merely of "economic liberty." For consider what is required in order to ensure that an overall distribution of wealth in a society fits a certain pattern. If the pattern requires distribution according to labor, need, or merit, this will require that government determine how hard-working, needy, or morally admirable each of the different members of society are relative to one another. Of course, it is highly implausible to suppose that this is possible even in principle: How precisely is a committee of bureaucrats to judge of such things, particularly when what counts as hard work or as a "need" is often highly subjective and dependent on individual circumstances, when there are deep disagreements in any society over what counts as moral merit, and when a person's overall character and genuine needs are extremely difficult to evaluate even *given* agreed-upon standards? In any event, if the state even tries to determine all this, obviously this will necessitate extensive snooping into individuals' personal lives, perhaps by involving employers, insurers, landlords, and the like in the task of collecting information on individual citizens' behavior and circumstances. It will also require, to make the task manageable in a diverse society, that a single set of standards of what counts as hard work, need, or merit simply be *imposed* by the state on all citizens, including those who do not agree with the standards (Hayek 1976).

That such an imposition is *actual* and not merely possible can be

74

seen from the recent history of attempts to apply egalitarian principles within Western democratic societies. Modern egalitarians have become preoccupied – indeed, some would say obsessed – with the topics of race, culture, sex, sexual orientation, disability, and the like, and to further the cause of equalizing the distribution of wealth have worked to infuse public education and the state regulation of business and private property with an ethos of "increased awareness" of – some would say hyper-sensitivity about – differences between individuals with respect to such things. In practice this has meant that employers, landlords, and business owners have been in effect forbidden by law (or at least by the threat of a lawsuit, which amounts to much the same thing) to use their own property in a way that accords with their own values, and that educators have been similarly forced to propagate the egalitarian ethos and to stifle the expression of views at odds with it. Opinions to the effect that, for example, some cultures are at least in some respects superior to others, that there are innate differences between the sexes, or that some sexual practices are abnormal or immoral, have come increasingly close to being effectively outlawed by the state – for anyone seeking to act on such opinions in his hiring or renting practices, or even to discuss and debate them in the context of the classroom, faces potential legal action and the loss of his livelihood, given developments in "civil rights" and "sexual harassment" law and the rise of "hate speech" codes, and given the increasing application of these laws and codes to more and more areas of everyday private life . And in some parts of the Western world – Canada and some countries within the European Union – the mere expression in speech or print of certain ideas on these matters has been *explicitly* outlawed. Egalitarianism has thus led – in practice, not just in theory – to the *imposition* on all of an ethic of "diversity," where all views and "lifestyles" *must*, according to *law*, be regarded by everyone as equally good (except, curiously, the view that *not* all views and lifestyles should be regarded as equally good).

That many readers would not find these developments troubling does not show that such developments do not in fact amount to a loss of liberty – it *might* show instead only that some people who would no doubt call themselves liberal and freedom-loving don't *really* mind the government imposing values on everyone in society, as long as it is *their* values that are imposed. But perhaps such people should consider what they would think if the shoe was on the other foot, and it was, say, the Christian Coalition determining what the distribution of wealth ought to be, whom employers could hire or fire, and what can be taught in the classroom – with a battery of lawyers ready to sue anyone who resisted into penury. Perhaps this thought experiment will indicate to them the dangers to liberty of allowing the state to impose a principle of distributive justice on society as a whole – and that just as liberty destroys patterns, so too do patterns destroy liberty, leading us down what Hayek famously called "the road to serfdom" (1944).

The critique of Rawls

Nozick applies his entitlement theory to a critique of the rival theory of John Rawls's *A Theory of Justice* (1971). In defending egalitarian liberalism, Rawls argues that the principles of justice that ought to govern society are precisely those that would be chosen by parties in what he calls the *original position*, a hypothetical "state of nature"-type situation in which individuals agree to a social contract behind a "veil of ignorance." What this means is that those making the agreement do not know anything about themselves that might bias their choice of principles – they are ignorant of their social status, income level, race, sex, special talents and abilities, and so forth. What they do know are very general facts about human nature, sociology, and the like, and that they want to make a choice of principles that will be in their own self-interest. The principles they will choose under these circumstances, Rawls holds, are these: the Liberty Principle, which guarantees the rights to life, liberty, property, freedom from arbitrary search and seizure, etc.; and the famous Difference Principle, which guarantees that "social and economic inequalities are to be arranged so that they are...to the greatest benefit of the least advantaged," entailing that any inequalities which do *not* benefit the least well-off members of society must be eliminated (1971, 83). This is usually interpreted as requiring the institution of a regime of continuous and extensive redistribution of wealth and the programs characteristic of the modern welfare state.

Nozick develops a number of detailed and penetrating objections to the presuppositions and execution of Rawls's project (1974, 183-231). Suffice it for us here to note that among the faults of that project, in Nozick's estimation, is that it commits a number of errors of the sort already described: The veil of ignorance, given that it excludes any knowledge about the actual concrete facts about human beings, including how they came to have what they have, "guarantees that end-state principles of justice will be taken as fundamental" (198-199) – the Difference Principle itself being such a principle (209) – and that holdings will be treated as if they fell like "manna from heaven" (199). It also treats, not only people's holdings, but even their natural talents

76

and abilities (and thus the wealth that flows from these), as a "collective asset" of society as a whole, to be harnessed by society in accord with the Difference Principle (Rawls 1971, 179) – thus violating self-ownership and the Kantian prohibition against using people as means (Nozick 1974, 228). Rawls justifies so treating natural abilities on the grounds that they are "arbitrary from a moral point of view" (Rawls 1971, 72), in that individuals, having been born with their abilities, did nothing to deserve them. Nor are a person's exertion of effort or the good character shown in developing and using his talents relevant, in Rawls's view, since these factors too are not to a person's credit, being the result, he claims, of upbringing and other circumstances outside the individual's control (104). But why, Nozick asks, is it necessarily relevant to whether I'm *entitled* to something that I *deserve* it (Nozick 1974, 225)? (You never *did* anything to deserve your eyeballs – but aren't you entitled to them nonetheless?) And how can "attributing *everything* noteworthy about the person completely to certain sorts of 'external' factors [and thus] denigrating a person's autonomy and prime responsibility for his actions" possibly serve to "buttress the dignity and self-respect of autonomous beings" that Rawls, like other egalitarians, claims to want to uphold (214)?

Taxation, forced labor, and theft

The point of the entitlement theory of justice is, as I've said, to show that justice does *not* in fact require a redistribution of wealth, and thus a more-than-minimal state. But Nozick also holds that justice in fact *forbids* a redistribution of wealth. It isn't merely that the state *needn't* redistribute wealth (as though this would be an admirable goal it nevertheless *may* engage in if it wishes to). It would in fact be unjust for it to do so. We've already seen in outline why this is so in chapter 3, but we now need to explore it in more detail – to explore, that is, the libertarian claim that redistributive taxation is inherently immoral.

Self-ownership vs. taxation

Nozick minces no words in objecting to taxation: "Taxation of earnings from labor is on a par with forced labor" (1974, 169). When you're forced to pay in taxes a percentage of what you earn from laboring, Nozick holds, you are in effect forced to labor for someone else, because the product of part of your labor is taken from you against your will and used for someone else's purposes (169-171; Feser 2000). Now perhaps you are not required to do a *specific kind* of labor, and can even choose whatever kind of labor you like. But how is that relevant? Even if you love pumping gas, if you pump it for three hours *for someone else's purposes*, and do so *involuntarily*, your labor has been forced; and a slave told by his master that he can choose between chopping wood, breaking rocks, painting the house, or painting a picture, wouldn't be any less a slave for that. Nor is it relevant that one could (unlike a typical slave) choose not to work at all, or at least could choose not to work beyond what is required to provide for basic needs, where only income made beyond that point is taxed. For the bottom line is still that *if* you work at all, or at least *if* you work beyond what is required for your basic needs, you will be *forced* to work *part* of that time for someone else, like "a horse harnessed to a wagon which doesn't *have* to move ever, but if it does, it must draw the wagon along" (1974, 229). If the taxes on eight hours labor amount to three hours worth of wages, then those three hours were hours you worked involuntarily for someone else's purposes. It's not as if you could avoid the taxes by working only five hours, for then the taxman will simply take instead the same percentage of the *five* hours labor – and trying to avoid paying those taxes by working fewer than five hours will have a similar result, as will trying to work any lesser number of hours to avoid paying the taxes.

Anyone who objects to forced labor, then, cannot consistently approve of taxation of labor. Some critics of Nozick, though, conceding that taxation amounts to something like forced labor, bite the bullet and suggest that perhaps a little forced labor is a good thing if its purpose is to realize some egalitarian redistribution of wealth, especially since the forced labor involved in taxation amounts to little more than a minor inconvenience (Wolff 1991, 92; Haworth 1994, 92). Now whether having 40-60% of your income taxed away (as it typically is in modern Western democracies) can fairly be represented as a *minor* inconvenience is, of course, open to doubt. But this response to Nozick errs, in any case, in assuming that inconvenience is what he is fundamentally concerned about. For the deeper point is that taxation of labor is simply inconsistent with the thesis of self-ownership, especially when motivated by end-result or patterned principles of justice or the requirements of funding the programs constitutive of the welfare state (Nozick 1974, 171-172). For in granting citizens an *entitlement* to certain services or to a share of "society's" wealth, such principles and programs in effect require that any time you labor, you must labor for the purposes of the state, or for the purposes of those who benefit from the state's largesse, since the state must redistribute part of the product of your labor to meet those

78

entitlements. Such principles and programs entail, that is, that the state and its beneficiaries have an entitlement or enforceable claim to, and thus a partial property right in, *your labor*, and thus in *you*. They are, in short, *part-owners of you*. The egalitarian welfare state thus amounts to a system of *slavery* – less onerous than *full* slavery, to be sure, but *partial* slavery is still slavery.

Some critics of Nozick (e.g. Kymlicka 1990, 107-118) allege that libertarian objections to taxation rest on a controversial Lockean theory of property rights, and thus have only as much force as such theories of property do. But it is important to notice that this argument of Nozick's does *not* rest on *any* particular theory of property rights; it depends only on the thesis of self-ownership itself (Feser 2000). Other critics of Nozick, preeminently G.A. Cohen, recognize this (Cohen 1995, chapter 9) – which is precisely why Cohen thinks it imperative for egalitarians to attempt to undermine self-ownership. As we argued in chapter 3, however, Nozick's critics have failed in this attempt.

"Taxation is theft"

Many libertarians *do* argue against taxation on the grounds that it violates property rights, however. Indeed, Nozick himself would so argue, on the grounds that taxation, being involuntary, violates the entitlement theory's principle of justice in transfer (Nozick 1974, 168). The point of the argument about forced labor and self-ownership is to give an argument against taxation that is *independent* of the property rights argument; but the property rights argument nevertheless remains. Taxation not only violates one's ownership of one's self, it violates one's ownership of his justly acquired property. As Rothbard puts it: "Taxation is theft, purely and simply, even though it is theft on a grand and colossal scale which no acknowledged criminals could hope to match. It is a compulsory seizure of the property of the State's inhabitants, or subjects" (1998, 162; see also Feser 2000; Feser 2001).

Note that it is irrelevant to the question of taxation's legitimacy that the state may use tax money for good causes, or even for your personal benefit. A mugger is still a thief even if he uses what he takes from your wallet for charitable purposes, and organized crime sometimes provides businesses genuine protection against small-time crooks in exchange for extorted payments. Nor is it relevant that one could always emigrate to avoid paying the taxes levied in a particular country: No one would think it a plausible defense of mafia extortion to say that those who are being extorted from can always move if they don't like it. It is also irrelevant that a tax may be supported by a majority of citizens who voted for it, since those who did *not* vote for it are as coerced into paying it as they would have been if they had no vote at all – after all, the state would hardly be justified in imprisoning, torturing, or killing an innocent person *simply* because a majority voted to have this done.

The widely (and uncritically) accepted notion that the will of a majority must always be followed – that as long as a policy was voted for by the people or their representatives, it is therefore legitimate – is one that Nozick attacks in what he calls "the Tale of the Slave" (1974, 290-292). Imagine you are a slave who is under the complete control of a cruel and arbitrary master. This is the usual picture of slavery, to which we all object. Now imagine a master who is kindlier, who punishes you only for clearly stated infractions and who gives you some free time. You are still a slave for all that, of course. But imagine next that the master has a group of slaves, and that he determines how to distribute things among them on the basis of moral grounds such as need, merit, hard work, etc; next, that he requires them to work only three days a week, letting them use the other days as they wish; further, that he eventually allows them instead to work for whomever and in whatever capacity they wish, requiring only that they pay him three-sevenths of their wages and that he be allowed to regulate certain dangerous activities that they engage in (e.g. smoking). Suppose he even allows the other slaves – 10,000 of them – to watch over you in his place, and they vote to decide what percentage of your earnings will be given to the master, what activities you can and cannot engage in, etc. In this case, Nozick says, "you now have 10,000 masters instead of just one; rather you have one 10,000-headed master. Perhaps the 10,000 even will be kindlier than [the one]. Still, they are your master" (291).

Now imagine that the 10,000, still having control over you, allow you to try to persuade them about how they should treat you; imagine further that at some point they actually allow you to vote in the very rare cases where their vote is deadlocked 5,000 to 5,000; finally, imagine that they eventually allow you to vote in all their proceedings – meaning that you have one vote in 10,001 concerning how much of your earnings are going to be taken from you, concerning what activities you will be allowed to engage in and under what conditions, and so forth. "The question is," Nozick says, "which transition [throughout all these stages] made it no longer the tale of a slave?" (292). Surely *no* transition did – you're as much a slave at the end of the process as at the beginning, though the slavery is now milder and partial. But what difference is there between your position at the end of this process and the position of a member of a democratic society? How does a society where what happens to you (including whether the rights you have as a self-owner will be respected) is determined by democratic vote any different from a society where you have 10,000 (or 10 million, or 100 million) masters?

Property rights

The critique of taxation as theft, unlike the argument about forced labor and self-ownership, might indeed seem to depend upon a controversial theory of property rights; and thus here, Nozick's critics often claim, there is a serious weakness in his position. For whatever Nozick says about just transfers of wealth, why (it is asked) should we assume that the more fundamental principle of just *acquisition* of previously unowned portions of the natural world gives people *absolute* property rights in those portions? Why can't we take at least *some* of it in taxes? Indeed, doesn't the Lockean Proviso require us to do so, given that "enough and as good" has clearly not been left for others to acquire, most if not all of the earth's natural resources having been acquired long ago? And should we really grant that the world is initially unowned in the first place? Don't we *all* collectively own it (Kymlicka 1990, 117-118)?

The first thing to note in response to such objections is that they are exasperatingly unspecific about what exactly it is they are supposed to show. Precisely how much taxation is entailed by these considerations, of what type and for what purposes? If the idea is that there ought to be taxation for the purposes of funding welfare programs for those destitute persons who have presumably been disadvantaged by violations of the Lockean Proviso, how are we to determine exactly who these persons are? After all, *most* people around today never had a chance to acquire previously unowned resources, yet most people are not destitute. Why assume that those who are destitute are destitute *because of* violations of the Lockean Proviso? (Maybe they would have been destitute in any case – perhaps the bad decisions or bad luck that led them to destitution in the actual world would have led them to destitution even in a world where they had a chance to acquire unowned resources.) Furthermore, even if this would justify taxation for welfare programs and the like, how would it justify government spending on arts and research, schools and museums, and all the other things egalitarians typically want government to fund? (Are we to suppose that all presently destitute people would have flocked to art exhibits if only they had had a chance to acquire land in the state of nature?) Moreover, how would it justify a strictly equal distribution of wealth, or distribution according to need, merit, or the like? And would it justify an income tax, a sales tax, or both? How about tariffs? And what *rate* of taxation, exactly? Thirty percent? Fifty percent? Sixty? (*Why?*) Not only do Nozick's egalitarian critics not *answer* such questions, they never even *consider* them.

In any case, such objections in fact have nothing like the force Nozick's critics assume them to have. To begin with, the notion that all of us collectively own all natural resources is a non-starter. For one thing, it is simply implausible: Are we really to suppose that we all collectively owned Greenland, say, before anyone set foot on it, or own the center of the earth now – or for that matter, that we all collectively own Pluto or the Andromeda galaxy? What would it *mean* to claim ownership, collective or otherwise, of places on which no one has in any way had any impact, or of places no one can even *get* to? If an individual person or corporation claimed ownership of the center of the earth, they'd be laughed at, and rightly so. But wouldn't the claim that *all* of us own it be equally laughable? Surely these claims are manifestly absurd, not because there is anything intrinsically absurd or unjust about ownership of the center of the earth – or of Pluto or Andromeda – per se, but rather because, given that no one currently has anything like the influence or power over such places that are in ordinary cases constitutive of ownership, there's *no sense* to be made of the suggestion that anyone (yet) owns them at all. Until someone *does something* with a resource, that is, it seems obvious that there can be no question of *anyone, either* collectively or privately, *owning* it.

Therein lies the intuitive plausibility of the Lockean theory that property results from someone "mixing his labor" with an unowned resource. Ownership of any sort can only get going when someone *makes it happen,* by *doing* something with a resource, with what is otherwise just an inert bit of stuff. But this always means some *individual* or group of individuals doing something – there's no such thing as all of us *collectively* "mixing our labor" with some unowned object. Of course, there are philosophical puzzles to be worked out here. As Nozick asks:

> [W]hy isn't mixing what I own with what I don't own a way of losing what I own rather than a way of gaining what I don't? If I own a can of tomato juice and spill it in the sea so that its molecules (made radioactive, so I can check this) mingle evenly throughout the sea, do I thereby come to own the sea, or have I foolishly dissipated my tomato juice? (1974, 174-175)

But such puzzles are not insurmountable. Surely the answer in this case is that I've lost my tomato juice, precisely because, as it's such a small fraction of the overall mixture that results, I cannot in any way be said to have done anything to the sea to alter it or bring it under my control. (Lightly blowing on a stick of wood instead of whittling it would seem similarly ineffective as a means of acquiring it, precisely because I haven't done anything to alter or control the wood.) "But what if instead you dump a *lake*-sized can of tomato juice into the sea – or a lake-sized can of fizzies, or nuclear waste that makes it glow green?" In these cases though, it seems quite plausible (or in any case not *absurd*, as the original tomato juice example was) to say that I *have* come to own the sea (provided no one else had any prior claim to it), precisely because I've so radically altered it. It is, in short, the tendency of labor mixing *significantly* to alter a resource or bring it under one's control that effectively turns it into property – but "all of us collectively" can't do this (in any case, we never have), only individuals and groups of individuals can.

In any case, it isn't clear why *collective* ownership is supposed by its advocates to be somehow less philosophically problematic than *private* ownership (Nozick 1974, 178); if anything it is *more* problematic, given that labor-mixing of some sort seems the only available way of getting property started, and that "all of us collectively" can't mix our labor. Furthermore, collective ownership of all natural resources would have morally intolerable consequences. As Cohen has argued, it seems to be incompatible with any robust conception of self-ownership, since even if I own myself, if external resources are collectively owned, I will be utterly dependent on (and virtually the slave of) everyone else, since I will be unable to use any of the world's resources, or even so much as move about the world, unless I first get the permission of everyone else in the world (1995, chapter 4). There are also, as we saw earlier, inevitable "tragedy of the commons" problems with collective ownership. When no one *in particular* owns something, no one in particular has any incentive to manage it wisely.

The Lockean Proviso

This last consideration sheds light on how we ought to understand the role of the Lockean Proviso. The point of the proviso, Nozick says, is "to ensure that the situation of others is not worsened" (1974, 175). But given the practical benefits of the institution of private property (some of which we noted in chapter 2) it is plausible that the situation of people in general has *not* been worsened by allowing initial acquisition (177). (This is, as Nozick goes on to say, *not* a utilitarian – as opposed to rights-based – defense of property, but rather merely grounds for holding that the Lockean Proviso has not been violated.)

Indeed, people's situation is in general *vastly better* as a result of some people's initially acquiring natural resources. As David Schmidtz points out:

> Philosophers who write on the subject of original appropriation tend to speak as if people who arrive first, and thus do all the appropriating, are much luckier than those who come later. The truth is, first appropriators begin the process of resource creation, while late-comers like ourselves get most of the benefits. Consider the Jamestown colony of 1607. Exactly what was it, we should ask, that made their situation so much better than ours? They never had to worry about being overcharged for car repairs. They never awoke in the middle of the night to the sound of noisy refrigerators, or leaky faucets, or flushing toilets. They never had to agonize over the choice of long-distance telephone companies. Are these the things that make us wish we had gotten there first? (1994, 45)

That we have the wealth and technology we have today – wealth and technology, along with all the conveniences they provide (and which we take for granted), of which our forefathers could not have dreamed – is the end result of a long process that only *began* with initial appropriation by those forefathers. *We*, and not they, are the more fortunate for their having "gotten there first." Those who came before us did the hard work of "taming the land" and, through their effort and ingenuity (and that of succeeding generations) making something out of it. Initial acquisition *only* depletes the stock of raw resources that can be *initially acquired*; as Schmidtz points out, it does *not* deplete the stock of *wealth* that can be *owned* (46). In fact, it *increases* that stock, as people *create* wealth with what they've acquired. "The lesson is that appropriation is not a zero-sum game. It is a positive-sum game" (46). Moreover, leaving resources unappropriated in the commons is itself not only *not* a positive-sum game, it is typically a *negative*-sum game. For the "tragedy of the commons" problem ensures that *unacquired* resources will be depleted, leaving everyone *worse off* (46-50). The Lockean Proviso thus not only allows for initial acquisition of unowned resources; in many cases, it actually *requires* it (48)!

Regarding appropriation, and transfers of wealth too, as zero-sum games – as if the stock of wealth in the world is like a pie with a finite number of pieces, where one person's getting a piece means that someone else won't get anything – is a notorious, and fallacious, tendency of egalitarian thinking. It is a fallacy also endemic to environmentalist thinking. We are these days used to hearing ever more frantic calls for "sustainable development" in the face of ever increasingly depleted natural resources. In fact, however, natural resources are in general *not* becoming depleted, as can be seen from the steady and continuous *decrease* in prices (in real dollars) over the decades for raw materials from iron ore to copper to natural gas. Contrary to popular opinion, forests are actually *increasing*, not decreasing – the one significant exception of the Amazon being a consequence of *Brazilian government subsidies*, not free market competition. Food is getting steadily more plentiful and varied, *except* in countries (e.g. the starvation-afflicted countries of sub-Saharan Africa) devoid of market competition and the rule of law.

Those who find such facts puzzling or paradoxical thus reveal their ignorance of economics. For the reason why resources are not generally decreasing, and are not likely to decrease in the foreseeable future, is that what *counts* as a resource and what can be *done with* a resource are determined by *human interests* and *human knowledge*. As technology advances in the context of (and as a consequence of) the competitive pressures of a free market, we are able to do more and better things, with lower cost and greater efficiency, and to do them using fewer resources, or with materials that once were nonexistent or used to seem worthless. Calculators that once were constructed out of tons of steel and miles of wire, that filled an entire room and cost hundreds of thousands of dollars, are now constructed out of plastic and silicon in a casing that fits in the palm of your hand, and are given away for free in cereal boxes. The "ultimate resource," as economist Julian Simon describes it, is *human ingenuity*, not the inert stuff we pull from the ground; and human ingenuity is limitless. (For detailed discussion of these issues, see Anderson and Leal 1991; Bailey 1993; Bailey 1995; Simon 1995; Simon 1996; Lomborg 2001. For an excellent brief discussion, see Narveson 1999, chapters 9 and 10).

Private property rights, far from depleting the resources available for future generations, radically *increase* these resources. And in allowing us to overcome "tragedies of the commons," they also provide the most reliable incentives for people not to pollute the environment: It simply doesn't pay to pollute your own property if maintaining it will bring larger returns in the long run, nor to pollute other people's property when they can retaliate through the legal system to what amounts to a violation of their rights (Nozick 1974, 79-81). It is no accident that the former states of the communist Eastern bloc, devoid of stable private property rights, were the scene of the greatest environmental devastation in history; nor is it an accident that it is precisely *government*-controlled lands that, in the Western world, tend to suffer the greatest pollution. (See again the references cited above.)

The burden of proof (again)

It seems, then, that, contrary to Nozick's critics, his Lockean account of initial acquisition can be readily defended. But perhaps Nozick has conceded too much to his critics in assuming that there really *is* in the first place a problem about whether the initial acquisition of private property can be just. For consider: To say that A committed an injustice against some other person B when he acquired a previously unowned resource R implies that B had some *right* over R that A violated. But B had no such rights, because *no one*, prior to A's acquisition, had any rights over R – it was, after all, previously unowned. But then the first person who *could* claim rights over R, the violation of which would constitute an injustice, is the person who first comes to appropriate R – which would, of course, be not B but A himself. B can have no grounds for complaint, then (de Jasay 1997, 171-176; Feser 2000; Feser forthcoming-b).

If this is correct, the upshot is that justice or injustice in holdings only comes into play *after* initial acquisition has already taken place; that is, it concerns *transfers* of holdings, *not* appropriations of holdings. Initial acquisition itself is as such *neither just nor unjust*. But then there is no question of needing to fulfill the Lockean (or any other) Proviso to guarantee just initial acquisition, and thus a just distribution. The *only* condition that must be fulfilled for a distribution to be just is that it fulfills the principle of justice in transfer – that is, that the transactions that gave rise to the distribution be voluntary. Taxation, being involuntary, is thus ruled out automatically, *whether or not* all initial acquisitions fulfilled the Lockean Proviso (apart, that is, from the taxation required to fund the minimal state – which, for the reasons discussed in chapter 4, doesn't quite count as taxation per se).

This doesn't mean that a person A might not act *immorally* after making an initial acquisition of previously unowned resources. For A to acquire the only water hole in a region and then refuse to allow travelers passing through to drink from it would of course be callous, cruel, and wicked. But the point is that it doesn't follow from that that it would be *unjust*, for not all moral duties are duties of justice. The travelers had no *right* to the water – it's *A's* water, after all – even though they *do* have grounds to accuse A of such vices as selfishness and greed. It is only violations of rights, however, and not violations of other moral duties, that could plausibly justify state intervention in the form of taxation (as opposed to moral censure by the community, which *would* be called for in this case). If I refuse to help you jump-start your car when you're late for work and I'm on my day off, I am guilty of selfishness and ought to be severely criticized by others for it; I am not, however, guilty of violating your rights in a way that would justify the state arresting me or taxing me to pay for replacing your dead battery.

It might be asked: "But what if other people – B, C, D, and E – were already using the water hole in common when it was acquired, and had come to depend on it?" But far from posing a problem for the account I'm suggesting, this scenario fits quite nicely into it. For if B, C, D, and E were already using the water hole in common, it seems to me that we should say that they had together *already* appropriated it themselves, in which case A would *not* be initially appropriating it, but stealing it. Many cases of resources existing "in the commons" are, I would argue, mischaracterized; they are in fact cases where appropriation *has* taken place, just not by a single individual. (True, this would be a kind of "collective appropriation," but it was initial appropriation *by society or mankind as a whole*, a group which has never in fact acted together to appropriate anything, that was rejected earlier as implausible, *not* initial appropriation by a group of specific individuals whose collective appropriative acts – in this case, bathing and washing in the water hole, drawing water from it, etc. – are readily identifiable.)

The fault with Nozick's account of distributive justice, then, may be not that it is too radically libertarian, but that it is not radical enough. For if the very question of justice, contrary to the assumption made by Nozick as much as by his critics, does not even arise until initial acquisition has already taken place – if it arises, that is, only where transfer is in question – then the burden of proof regarding private property is, like the burden of proof regarding self-ownership, clearly on Nozick's opponent. *No one* had any claim to R at all until A appropriated it. So obviously the default assumption is that A has a right to it. And that means an "absolute right": For how, given that A is the first to have *any* right *at all* over R, could he have the right to *use* R but not, say, to sell it or destroy it? What is it exactly that keeps him from having those latter rights, if not someone else's competing claim over R – when, by hypothesis, there *are no* other such claims? It is not

A who needs to justify his exclusive use of R. It is rather those who want to take R from him who need to justify themselves.

The way these matters are often discussed simply disguises these facts, and begs the question against the libertarian. People say things like "Why should we allow people to have an absolute right to their property? Why can't we take some of it in taxes?'' But where exactly do people who ask such things get the idea that it is up to *them* to "allow" this in the first place? Doesn't putting the question this way implicitly *assume* that "we" have the *right* to decide whether or not people can keep their holdings – which is precisely what is at issue? And *who* exactly are meant by "we," anyway? The whole of society? (In which case, where do these people get the right to speak for *all* of us?) Or does "we" only mean "those of us who approve of redistributive taxation"? (In which case, why should those of us who do *not* approve of it care what *they* think?)

The institution of private property, as we've argued and as all of human history attests, is a precondition of both political liberty and economic prosperity (Bethell 1998; Pipes 1999). It is thus prima facie morally justified, *whatever* one thinks of the argument of this section. But that too puts the burden of proof on the defender of taxation. For taxation involves at the very least a *weakening* of property rights, and thus the weakening of an institution that we are morally bound to preserve. It is incumbent on anyone who advocates such a weakening, then, to justify his doing so; he cannot reasonably assume the burden of proof to fall on his opponent. No reasonable person, after all, would say that we ought to be allowed to kill people at will unless it is proved that some particular killing is unjustified. The right to life puts the burden of proof on the *killer*, to produce a good reason for killing (e.g. self-defense). Why is the right to property any different? How can advocates of redistributive taxation so blithely accuse Nozick (falsely, as we've seen) of presenting a "libertarianism without foundations" when the burden of proof is surely on *them* to justify their redistributive schemes in the first place? Where do they get off arrogantly *assuming* that our property is *theirs* to do with as they wish until we can prove otherwise?

These questions, like some of the others raised in this chapter, are rarely considered (much less answered) by Nozick's critics. For them to raise them, however, would be for them to acknowledge a burden of proof which, if what has been said in this chapter is correct, they cannot meet. The right to property, like the right to self-ownership, is inviolable. To recognize this is to grasp the first principle, indeed the *only* principle, of justice in the political sphere.

6

The Best of All Possible Worlds

Utopia

That last line of the last chapter no doubt scandalizes many readers, as does the conception of politics it evinces. "Surely there is more to morality than property rights, and more to social life than exchanging property!" they might be tempted to respond; "And surely there is more to community than the collective safeguarding of that property! What a cold and heartless – indeed, positively counter-utopian – conception of human life is embodied by such a view!"

They would, of course, be absolutely right to think this. Where they go wrong is in assuming that Nozick would think, or is required by his position to think, any differently – in assuming that Nozick's *political* philosophy is intended to be a complete *social* philosophy. They go wrong also in assimilating "morality" to justice, "social life" to politics, and "community" to government. For justice is not the whole of morality; not all of social life is politics; and genuine human community definitely is *not* the same thing as government action.

Justice – the securing of which is the chief end of political action – is, however important, but one virtue among others. Sometimes what is called "justice" is not justice at all, but a mask for something decidedly unvirtuous, such as envy. One suspects that the demand for equality is a case in point; certainly one suspects this when one considers that equality as an ideal is rarely *argued* for by its proponents, and is almost *never* argued for very *well* (Nozick 1974, chapter 8). There are, in any case, virtues that are as important as justice, and some that are *more* important. Temperance, prudence, fortitude, faith, hope, and love are cases in point, and only a fool could believe that the practice of these virtues will be guaranteed if only we hit upon the right government program.

Government itself, however high-flown the rhetoric often spouted in its defense, is, it must always be remembered, nothing more than *brute force*, the getting of people to do things or to refrain from doing things by the threat of violence. Sometimes, as when the defense of individual rights is involved, such force is necessary; it remains force nonetheless. And when it involves the imposition of redistributive taxation or paternalistic regulation, it involves nothing more than *some* people forcing *other* people – innocent people who have violated no one else's rights – to do things against their will, to *submit* to the will of those doing the forcing. *Whether or not* one thinks such arm-twisting is morally justified, it is dishonest, indeed perverse, to talk smugly as if it is the quintessence of "community." Nor can politics – which in a non-libertarian society amounts to little more than the struggle to be the ones who get to force the others, even if "for their own good" – plausibly be regarded as a paradigmatically *social* activity, at least not if "social" is meant to connote an ideal of high-minded cooperation.

A conception of human life that sees all questions of morality, and indeed everything of value, as necessarily entailing a political program backed by the police power of the state and the threat of litigation, is one that can only be described, charitably, as deficient; less charitably, as warped. We need, in Nozick's view, to learn "to see through the political realm" (1974, x). We need to get beyond the tendency – a very modern tendency that would have surprised earlier generations – reflexively to think of all problems as having a political solution, of all progress as dependent on government action. We need in particular to stop thinking in utopian terms – or rather, to stop thinking of utopia in political terms. The utopias of the past have usually been implemented in a political fashion, and they have universally failed, often catastrophically – think the French Revolution, Auschwitz, the Gulag Archipelago. They have also involved the imposition of *one* group's vision of utopia on *everyone* (indeed, this is part of the reason why they have failed). If utopian thinking is to be realistic and to have a future, it must avoid these errors.

The Framework

The minimal state allows us to do just this, Nozick argues; it provides a "framework for utopia" (1974, 297) within which individuals and groups can work out, free of interference by others or by the state, their own utopian visions in a *voluntary* fashion. It embodies the truth that "utopia is meta-utopia: the environment in which utopian experiments may be tried out; the environment in which people are free to do their own thing; the environment which must, to a great extent, be realized first if more particular utopian visions are to be realized stably" (312).

Part of the reason for this is that it allows us to avoid the danger of finding ourselves stuck with a scheme that turns out not to be so workable after all: If different people are allowed to try different things, with no one group being allowed to force everyone to accept, once and for all, its vision of the ideal society, we'll be more likely to see what works and what doesn't, and avoid the catastrophe of finding out only after it's too late that we've committed ourselves to a mistaken set of assumptions about how the world works. But another part of the reason is that, whatever the objective facts about what will work and what won't, there are also in Nozick's view questions of value that simply cannot be settled objectively:

> Wittgenstein, Elizabeth Taylor, Bertrand Russell, Thomas Merton, Yogi Berra, Allen Ginsburg, Harry Wolfson, Thoreau, Casey Stengal, The Lubavitcher Rebbe, Picasso, Moses, Einstein, Hugh Hefner, Socrates, Henry Ford, Lenny Bruce, Baba Ram Dass, Gandhi, Sir Edmund Hillary, Raymond Lubitz, Buddha, Frank Sinatra, Columbus, Freud, Norman Mailer, Ayn Rand, Baron Rothschild, Ted Williams, Thomas Edison, H.L. Mencken, Thomas Jefferson, Ralph Ellison, Bobby Fischer, Emma Goldman, Peter Kropotkin, you, and your parents. Is there really *one* kind of life which is best for all of these people?...The idea that there is...one best society for *everyone* to live in seems to me to be an incredible one. (And the idea that, if there is one, we now know enough to describe it is even more incredible.) (310)

The reason why this is incredible is because of the disagreement that obviously exists between the people Nozick names, and between all of us, over what is the best way of life. Some of these disagreements may in principle be capable of being settled rationally; but does that mean that, until they are, one group can force its opinions on everyone else? (*Which* group? Why *them*?) Other disagreements seem impossible to settle, precisely because they depend on ineliminable differences in experiences, talents, aptitudes, and interests. (And why would we want to eliminate these differences even if we could?)

The beauty of the minimal state is that it doesn't require these differences to be settled. Every individual and group is free to set up whatever arrangements it likes, so long as they do not force everyone else to go along. *And this includes non-libertarians.* It is usually thought that libertarianism itself *requires* that everyone live according to a laissez faire capitalist ethos, but that isn't so. *Some* individuals within the context of a minimal state may want to do this, of course, and opt to participate, say, in a community that seeks to emulate the freewheeling entrepreneurs of Galt's Gulch in Ayn Rand's *Atlas Shrugged.* But others may prefer to set up a socialist society or a hippie commune, while yet others opt instead for a morally austere Puritan commonwealth or Buddhist *sangha* or Muslim *umma.* In a sense, then, libertarianism doesn't even require that people accept the minimal state as the optimal political system! For people are free to set up, within its boundaries, quasi-states of whatever size and degree of intervention in people's lives they wish, *provided that* people are allowed *voluntarily* either to submit themselves, or refuse to submit, to such more-than-minimal quasi-states. *All* of these societies will be possible within the larger, encompassing framework of the libertarian minimal state.

That, in effect, is in Nozick's view a further argument for the minimal state, independent of the argument from individual rights. For libertarianism alone makes possible the realization in principle of *everyone's* vision of what society should be. It thus provides the only common ground on the basis of which individuals and communities with radically different values can live together in peace. No other political philosophy does this, *including* liberalism, which typically prides itself on its purported tolerance for diversity. For libertarianism, unlike liberalism, does not *force* you to "*celebrate* diversity," to admit into your restaurant or apartment complex or organizations people you don't like or whose moral code you disagree with, to pay for public schools whose curriculum you find offensive and teachers you find incompetent, or even to keep your religious or other values out of public life, broadly construed. It requires only that you *leave people alone who don't agree with you.* If group A goes in for drug use and free love, heterosexual, homosexual or what have you, fine; A can set up a community that fosters these things, that requires its members to pay for clean needles and free prophylactics, and other communities can't stop them. But if group B requires *its* members to abstain from sex outside of heterosexual marriage, to swear off drugs and to follow the teachings of the Church, then they can set up *their* community too, and no one can stop *them*. Each community can preach to the members of the other if the others are willing to listen, and try to convince them to defect; but they cannot *coerce* members of the other group to give up their preferred ways, nor can they force members of the other group to support the propagation of their *own* views. B can't force members of A to go to Sunday school or to fund the distribution of Bibles; A can't force the members of B to send their employees to multicultural sensitivity training or to fund the distribution of condoms. *True* tolerance is a two-way street – it requires those who claim to be "tolerant" and "open-minded" not to force *others* to be; it leaves open the possibility that what some people consider tolerance and open-mindedness, other people have a right to regard as a collapse of ethical and intellectual standards.

Some critics of Nozick acknowledge the attractiveness of this proposal, but suggest that it isn't as fair to all points of view as it sounds: For wouldn't members of a socialist society constantly be tempted to flee to a neighboring capitalist society, with its greater individual wealth? Wouldn't people who decide to give up such a life (and thus sell their communally held land) find it difficult to come back to it (due to a rise in land prices) should they change their minds yet again? (Wolff 1991, 135). But surely this sort of objection is rather pathetic – a complaint to the effect that "If we let everyone *choose* what sort of utopia they'd like to live in, they might not choose the way *I'd* like them to!" But so what? (Presumably purveyors of Nazi and Communist "utopias" would find it difficult to attract many Jews or "bloodsucking capitalists" to enter into their villages and voluntarily agree to be liquidated. Should we feel sorry for them on that account?) Why should we expect that *every* utopian experiment will be able to get off the ground? *No* political philosophy could guarantee that. But libertarianism at least allows everyone to *try* to attract people to participate in their utopian experiments. It allows even the socialist and liberal egalitarian to make a go of their proposals. By contrast, the socialist or liberal would *forbid* laissez faire capitalists even the *chance* to do this. So how can he legitimately complain that his vision might not work in a situation where people could freely choose or reject it? (If that's true, isn't it reason to think it might *not* be such a terrific vision after all?)

And suppose that certain experiments *do* fail, that in a context where people are forbidden to force their views on others by threat of violence, some conceptions naturally tend to die out and others to thrive. Wouldn't this be a *good* thing? Wouldn't it give us solid *evidence* concerning which visions are workable and which are not? And if, as proponents of the kind of Hayekian cultural evolution discussed earlier would predict, such a "filter device" (as Nozick calls it (312-317)) would tend to leave as the most thriving communities those which combine free markets with a family-oriented moral conservatism (Hayek 1988), wouldn't this be a strong indication that such a combination may be the optimal one for human beings? Wouldn't it provide a powerful case for the conclusion that a "bourgeois capitalist" society really is, if not the *only* possible world (since there would no doubt always exist on the fringes of that society a few bohemians who stubbornly refuse to conform), nevertheless the *best* of all possible worlds? (Could a fear that this would indeed be the result of Nozick's framework for utopia provide an explanation of why some are so hostile to it?)

Whatever the correct answers are to these questions, Nozick allows us seriously to ask them in a way his opponents do not. Social engineers and political activists frequently *talk* about experimentation, new ideas, etc.; but they often seem less keen on actually *allowing* such things whenever they conflict with their own visions of how life ought to be lived. Similarly, they talk grandly about "freedom" and "human rights," while *denying* anyone the right or freedom to disagree with or opt out of *their* conceptions of how society ought to be ordered. Nozick challenges us to match our practice to our rhetoric, to have the honesty and courage to face up to what a respect for the dignity of the individual as free, inviolate, a self-owner and an end-in-himself, truly entails. "How *dare* any state or group of individuals do more. Or less." (Nozick 1974, 334)

94

Bibliography

Works by Robert Nozick

Nozick, Robert. 1974. *Anarchy, State, and Utopia.* New York: Basic Books.

-------. 1981. *Philosophical Explanations.* Cambridge, Mass.: Belknap Press.

-------. 1986. "Robert Nozick." *The Harvard Guide to Influential Books: 113 Distinguished Harvard Professors Discuss the Books That Have Helped to Shape Their Thinking.* New York: Harper and Row.

-------. 1989. *The Examined Life: Philosophical Meditations.* New York: Simon and Schuster.

-------. 1990. *The Normative Theory of Individual Choice.* Garland Press. [Reprint of 1963 Ph.D. dissertation.]

-------. 1993. *The Nature of Rationality.* Princeton, NJ: Princeton University Press.

-------. 1997. *Socratic Puzzles.* Cambridge, Mass.: Harvard University Press.

-------. 2001. *Invariances: The Structure of the Objective World.* Cambridge, Mass.: Belknap Press.

Works about Robert Nozick

Borradori, Giovanna. 1994. *The American Philosopher: Conversations with Quine, Davidson, Putnam, Nozick, Danto, Rorty, Cavell, MacIntyre, and Kuhn.* Chicago: University of Chicago Press.

Cohen, G.A. 1995. *Self-Ownership, Freedom, and Equality.* New York: Cambridge University Press.

Hailwood, Simon A. 1996. *Exploring Nozick: Beyond Anarchy, State, and Utopia.* Sydney: Avebury.

Lacey, A.R. 2001. *Robert Nozick.* Acumen Publishing Ltd.

Nagel, Thomas. 1981. "Libertarianism Without Foundations." In Paul 1981.

Paul, Jeffrey, ed. 1981. *Reading Nozick: Essays on Anarchy, State, and Utopia.* Totowa, NJ: Rowman and Littlefield.

Rothenberg, Randall. 1983. "Philosopher Robert Nozick vs. Philosopher John Rawls." *Esquire* March: 201-209.

Sanchez, Julian. 2001. "Interview with Robert Nozick." *LaissezFaireBooks.com* (August 30)

Schmidtz, David, ed. 2002. *Robert Nozick.* New York: Cambridge University Press.

Wolff, Jonathan. 1991. *Robert Nozick: Property, Justice, and the Minimal State.* Stanford, CA: Stanford University Press.

Works about libertarianism

Barnett, Randy. 1998. *The Structure of Liberty: Justice and the Rule of Law.* New York: Oxford University Press.

Benson, Bruce L. 1990. *The Enterprise of Law: Justice Without the State.* San Francisco: Pacific Research Institute.

Boaz, David, ed. 1997. *The Libertarian Reader.* New York: The Free Press.

Buchanan, James M. 1975. *The Limits of Liberty: Between Anarchy and Leviathan.* Chicago: University of Chicago Press.

Conway, David. 1995. *Classical Liberalism: The Unvanquished Ideal.* New York: St. Martin's Press.

De Jasay, Anthony. 1997. *Against Politics.* New York: Routledge.

Feser, Edward. 1997. "Hayek on Social Justice: Reply to Lukes and Johnston." *Critical Review* 11:581-606.

-------. 1998. "Hayek, Social Justice, and the Market: Reply to Johnston." *Critical Review* 12: 269-281.

-------. 2000. "Taxation, Forced Labor, and Theft." *The Independent Review* 5:219-235.

-------. 2001. "Taxation, Forced Labor, and Theft: Reply to Edwards." *The Independent Review* 6:259-262.

-------. forthcoming-a. "Hayek on Tradition." *The Journal of Libertarian Studies.*

-------. forthcoming-b. "There Is No Such Thing As An Unjust Initial Acquisition." *Social Philosophy and Policy.*

Friedman, David. 1989. *The Machinery of Freedom: Guide to a Radical Capitalism,* 2nd ed. La Salle, Illinois: Open Court.

Friedman, Milton. 1962. *Capitalism and Freedom.* Chicago: University of Chicago Press.

Haworth, Alan. 1994. *Anti-libertarianism.* New York: Routledge.

Hayek, F.A. 1944. *The Road to Serfdom.* Chicago: University of Chicago Press.

-------. 1948. *Individualism and Economic Order.* Chicago: University of Chicago Press.

-------. 1960. *The Constitution of Liberty.* Chicago: University of Chicago Press.

-------. 1976. *Law, Legislation, and Liberty, Volume 2: The Mirage of Social Justice.* Chicago: University of Chicago Press.

-------. 1988. *The Fatal Conceit: The Errors of Socialism.* Chicago: University of Chicago Press.

Lester, J.C. 2000. *Escape From Leviathan: Liberty, Welfare and Anarchy Reconciled.* New York: St. Martin's Press.

Lomasky, Loren. 1987. *Persons, Rights, and the Moral Community.* New York: Oxford University Press.

Machan, Tibor. 1989. *Individuals and Their Rights.* La Salle, Illinois: Open Court.

Machan, Tibor R. and Douglas B. Rasmussen, eds. 1995. *Liberty for the 21ˢᵗ Century.* Lanham, Maryland: Rowman and Littlefield.

Mack, Eric. 1981. "How to Derive Libertarian Rights." In Paul 1981.

-------. 1995. "Moral Individualism and Libertarian Theory." In Machan and Rasmussen 1995.

Mises, Ludwig von. 1951. *Socialism: An Economic and Sociological Analysis,* 2ⁿᵈ ed. New Haven: Yale University Press.

-------. 1978. *Liberalism: A Socio-Economic Exposition.* Kansas City: Sheed, Andrews, and McMeel, Inc.

Narveson, Jan. 1988. *The Libertarian Idea.* Philadelphia: Temple University Press.

-------. 1999. *Moral Matters,* 2ⁿᵈ ed. Peterborough, Ontario: Broadview Press.

Rand, Ayn. 1957. *Atlas Shrugged.* New York: Random House.

-------. 1966. *Capitalism: The Unknown Ideal.* New York: New American Library.

Rasmussen, Douglas B. and Douglas J. Den Uyl. 1991. *Liberty and Nature.* La Salle, Illinois: Open Court.

Rothbard, Murray. 1973. *For a New Liberty.* New York: Macmillan.

-------. 1998. *The Ethics of Liberty.* New York: New York University Press.

Schmidtz, David. 1994. "The Institution of Property." *Social Philosophy and Policy* 11: 42-62.

Sciabarra, Chris. 2000. *Total Freedom: Toward a Dialectical Libertarianism.* University Park: Pennsylvania State University Press.

Smith, Tara. 1995. *Moral Rights and Political Freedom.* Lanham, Maryland: Rowman and Littlefield.

Spencer, Herbert. 1995. *Social Statics.* New York: Robert Schalkenbach Foundation.

Other works cited

Anderson, Terry L. and Donald R. Leal. 1991. *Free Market Environmentalism.* San Francisco: Pacific Research Institute.

Bailey, Ronald. 1993. *Eco-Scam*. New York: St. Martin's Press.

-------, ed. 1995. *The True State of the Planet*. New York: The Free Press.

Beck, Lewis White, ed. 1988. *Kant Selections*. New York: Macmillan.

Beito, David. 2000. *From Mutual Aid to the Welfare State*. University of North Carolina Press.

Bethell, Tom. 1998. *The Noblest Triumph: Property and Prosperity Through the Ages*. New York: St. Martin's Press.

Buchanan, James M. and Gordon Tullock. 1962. *The Calculus of Consent*. Ann Arbor: University of Michigan Press.

Courtois, Stephane et al., eds. 1999. *The Black Book of Communism*. Cambridge: Harvard University Press.

Kukathas, Chandran and Philip Pettit. 1990. *Rawls: A Theory of Justice and its Critics*. Stanford, CA: Stanford University Press.

Kymlicka, Will. 1990. *Contemporary Political Philosophy: An Introduction*. Oxford: Clarendon Press.

Locke, John. 1963. *Two Treatises of Government*. Peter Laslett, ed. Cambridge: Cambridge University Press.

Lomborg, Bjorn. 2001. *The Skeptical Environmentalist*. New York: Cambridge University Press.

Morse, Jennifer Roback. 2001. *Love and Economics: Why the Laissez-Faire Family Doesn't Work*. Dallas: Spence Publishing.

Murray, Charles. 1994. *Losing Ground: American Social Policy 1950-1980*, 2nd ed. New York: Basic Books.

Pipes, Richard. 1999. *Property and Freedom*. New York: Knopf.

Rawls, John. 1971. *A Theory of Justice*. Cambridge, Mass.: Belknap Press.

Rector, Robert. 1998. "The Myth of Widespread American Poverty." *Heritage Foundation Backgrounder* No. 1221 (Sept. 18)

Scruton, Roger. 2000. *An Intelligent Person's Guide to Modern Culture*. South Bend, Indiana: St. Augustine's Press.

Simon, Julian L., ed. 1995. *The State of Humanity*. Oxford: Blackwell.

-------. 1996. *The Ultimate Resource 2*. Princeton: Princeton University Press.

Sowell, Thomas. 1993. *Inside American Education*. New York: The Free Press.

Sullum, Jacob. 1998. *For Your Own Good: The Anti-Smoking Crusade and the Tyranny of Public Health*. New York: The Free Press.